Guide Me Through This Barren Land

Guide Me Through This Barren Land

A Devotional for the Childless Woman

Vicki Caswell

Pleasant Word
A Division of WINEPRESS PUBLISHING

Pleasant Word (a division of WinePress Publishing, PO Box 428, Enumclaw, WA 98022) functions only as book publisher. As such, the ultimate design, content, editorial accuracy, and views expressed or implied in this work are those of the author.

ISBN 1-4141-0378-6
Library of Congress Catalog Card Number: 2005900556

Dedication

For Ed,

the love of my life,

and for Gail Benn,

sky-painter.

Table of Contents

Foreword

It's a club no member wanted to join. And it's a big club—more than six million strong!

You know the one I mean: *The Infertility Club.* If you belong, you won't actually carry a membership card, but you'll probably have some—*if not all*—of the identifying characteristics:

- You dread Mother's Day more than April 15, the tax-filing deadline.
- You consider these two words the most profane in the English language: "Just relax."
- You know what HSG stands for and you can pronounce it correctly.
- You fantasize about spending your Christmas bonus (not on a new car or trip to Tahiti, but) on an IVF cycle.

- You wonder about injustice when the wombs of those who don't appreciate kids resemble the Fertile Crescent while your own is more like Death Valley.

You are not alone. And though you may identify less with the fertility of Hagar than with the infertility of her rival, Sarah, you can appreciate what Hagar called the Lord when she was languishing alone in the wilderness: *El Roi*, "the God who sees."

After awhile you come to see that *El Roi* is with you every moment—through every test, every insensitive word endured, and those sleepless, tear-filled nights. He does see…and He *does* care for you.

This book is about that care. Written by an infertility patient who has been thrown for many loops, *Guide Me Through This Barren Land* reminds readers of God's love from someone intimately acquainted with the wild, seemingly endless ride. My dear friend, Vicki Caswell, is as warm on paper as she is in person. And her life matches her words. Here she shares the pain and the hopes, the laughter and tears, the lows and highs of the roller coaster of infertility. She brings to her subject the unique perspective of a woman whose God is strapped in next to her for the long and often perilous ride.

From Mother's Day meditations to raps about IVF, the devotional thoughts in this book will direct you to what is true, honorable, and right while you live in a world full of lies, shame, and ugliness.

Sometimes the author's ponderings will even make you laugh. And whereas infertility's hope is often accompanied by disappointment, the kind of hope offered here never disappoints. So, in the end, these meditations do even more than help people learn how to endure the crushing blows of infertility. They teach us how to live.

—**Sandra Glahn, Th.M.**, author, *When Empty Arms Become a Heavy Burden* and *The Infertility Companion*

Acknowledgments

Thanks to the Maranatha Christian Writer's Conference Staff for conceiving the idea for this book. Also, I want to thank my original editing team for their good suggestions and the time spent pouring over the original drafts of the manuscript: Gail Benn (thanks for putting up with me all these years), Gail Shaw (you provided the laptop and constant encouragement), Polly Lott (your tears inspired me), Diane Farmer (you remain a constant in my life), Knute Larson (thank you, sir; your signed copy is on the way). I am especially and humbly grateful to the editor extraordinaire, Sandra Glahn (sisters of warpedness forever) for her time and talent.

Special heartfelt thanks to: Gail Benn. This book became reality because of you. Before I met you, I believe… on my darkest day of depression… in the deepest grip of infertility, God whispered a promise: "I'm sending you Gail." Though I didn't quite catch what He said, a seed of strength was implanted in my heart. You've helped me journey to a place of purpose and contentment.

Gail Shaw: You never stopped believing in the reality of this book, and you never let me cast it aside. I admire and respect you to no end.

Heidi Meares: My sister in the "club no one wants to join." Your gift of encouragement is phenomenal. In what God has entrusted you to endure, sister, it is clear that He's building something amazing in you.

Sandi Glahn and William Cutrer (Dr. Bill): Your book, *When Empty Arms Become a Heavy Burden*, was the single most vital part of my path to contentment. My tears were different after reading it, and a glimmer of hope was born.

Emily Lyon: My "pseudodaughter." From the shy high school freshman to a confident, spiritually thriving college woman. You bring out the "animated" in me!

Matthew and Heather Mitchell and Emily Miller: "Mattman and H.G." You are so very dear to my heart. Lil' E., I'll soon teach you how to cross your eyes. Thanks Michelle and Steve, "T." and Tom for sharing these sweet little characters with me.

Mom and Dad, you believed I could do it!

And my deepest depth of gratitude goes to my dear husband, Ed. You helped get my writer's office together and cheered me on through the long, arduous process. ("Aren't you done yet?") And you made the dedication page after all (hee hee). Thank you for your committed love. What a man! You would've been a tremendous father.

Preface

This book came from my own personal journey through infertility. And yet, its existence came into being due to a deeper need—that of a spiritual journey. We all face trials of some form and at some level; no one escapes the fierce wrath of life. My miscarriage in 1995 was a turning point for me. Until that time, no serious difficulty had touched me personally. Certainly I had faced trials, but mostly I'd suffered because of things that happened to *others* around me. It was through my miscarriage that I knew I had finally joined the "Crisis Club." And after that, the infertility struggle began.

A friend said recently: "You may not birth a baby, but you're going to birth a book." And another friend said after reading my manuscript: "This is your firstborn." They got it right! That is how I feel about bringing forth this book—labor pains and all!

I felt that a story like this needed to be on the bookstore shelves. I know many infertile couples are in great turmoil, but they keep their silence. May this book help them find a voice with which to express their feelings to others. In writing this, I also hope to educate those who walk closely with infertile couples in order to help them understand how to help and to understand the depth of their suffering.

Mostly, though, I want this book to be my way of entering the home of a childless woman, bringing hope and comfort and a hug, and tenderly whispering, "Come here, sister, don't you hate this pain? I do, too. But with God's help, you'll make it."

— Vicki Caswell
3145 Rockingham Street
Uniontown, Ohio 44685
www.vcaswell.com
vicki@vcaswell.com

PART ONE

Manifold Emotions: What Your Heart Must Endure

"Infertility isn't a state; it's a journey—
a painful and sometimes long journey through
places you never thought you'd have to go."

—Marlo Schalesky,
from Empty Womb, Aching Heart

"I cry out to you, O God, but you do not answer;
I stand up, but you merely look at me.
The churning inside me never stops;
days of suffering confront me."

—Job 30:20, 27

Infertility is an unexpected explosion in a world where having children is a natural and common thing. There are a myriad of emotions that an infertile woman must deal with as she daily faces images of motherhood—anger, jealousy, depression, disillusionment, confusion, trying to be joyful for others, feeling abandoned, cursed, punished by God....

Day One

Guide Me

"They will feed beside the roads and find pasture on every barren hill.... He who has compassion on them will guide them and lead them beside springs of water."

—Isaiah 49:9–10

I work at a church and during a staff meeting, just for fun, a huge slide of an ultrasound image was displayed to celebrate the announcement of a new pregnancy. Talk about having my inadequacy thrown in my face! It was devastating to see this enormous picture of a child in a womb projected before all present.

Then, in a surreal moment known only to me, the next slide was a big, red "X." To everyone else it was a technical blooper, but I wanted to shout out: "And that's a picture of my *no children!*"

I knew Satan was taunting me, beating me with his sucker punches. I wanted to just get up and run! But I didn't run. God kept me in my seat.

Next we sang a hymn. And with the Lord's mighty power, He beat Satan down as I was strengthened by the magnitude of these words:

Guide me, O Thou great Jehovah,
Pilgrim through this barren *land,*

I am weak, but Thou art mighty,
Hold me with Thy powerful Hand!

The message could not have been any clearer if ten thousand angels had delivered it. Great Jehovah showed His mighty power and awesome love to me that day.

I reach for the Lord's powerful Hand as He guides me through this barren land...

Bearing Fruit

God spoke to me so powerfully in that song. He promised to guide me through this barren land. And He has. And He is. He will guide you through your barren land, also. Your choice to follow Him may just be beginning as you read this devotional. Take His Hand, won't you, and come....

Day Two

Waiting

"Jesus said, 'This sickness will not end in death. No, it is for God's glory so that God's Son may be glorified through it.' Jesus loved Martha and her sister and Lazarus. Yet when he heard that Lazarus was sick, he stayed where he was two more days."

—John 11:4–6

Today I wait.

The Lord seems to tarry in granting life to my womb, but I trust in His sovereign timing. He teaches me to trust and wait. *Waiting* is the definitive word in childlessness. Especially in those few weeks between ovulation and the telltale sign of non-conception or conception.

Mary, Martha, and Lazarus were dear friends to Jesus. When Lazarus became seriously ill, it made sense for his sisters to send for Jesus' help. They trusted in His love.

Like Martha and Mary I treasure my relationship with Jesus and believe He cares deeply. These sisters knew that if they called on Him, He would be there. And yet those words from the verse seem to jump out to me now: "He stayed where he was *two more days*" (italics mine).

What? Shouldn't the Lord be rushing to our aid in the event of such an emergency? But Christ's words reveal the deeper truth of waiting: "It is for God's glory."

When Jesus arrived on the scene, by all appearances He was too late. Lazarus was dead. But the Lord Jesus was not confined to the physical laws of this world. He miraculously raised Lazarus from the dead, and in so doing gave a deeper message: Those who trust in Him will have eternal life.

As Martha and Mary did when Lazarus lay four days in the tomb, I will pray and ponder if there is life. Only instead of a tomb, I pray concerning my womb. Jesus is Life, and He has given me eternal life. I wait to see His glory.

Martha and Mary did not understand at first why Jesus waited in coming to them, but the result of their extended wait was the birth of renewed trust.

If I am not pregnant, let me hang my head in disappointment for a moment, then let me lift my head in trust and hope for an eternity.

I wait.

Bearing Fruit

In those maddening days before discovering if you are or are not pregnant, do things you enjoy. This will help take your mind off the wait and will build your attitude to a positive level before the (potential) drop due to disappointment in—again—not being pregnant.

Day Three

Eighteen Ways to Make a Baby

"I will instruct you and teach you in the way you should go;
I will counsel you and watch over you."

—Psalm 32:8

Infertility is a painful pilgrimage with many pathways to travel. Now, with all the miraculous and sometimes scary techniques available in the quest of fertility, it can feel overwhelming.

I was amazed to discover that, besides natural intercourse, there are eighteen additional ways to make a baby! These include: artificial insemination (AI) with a husband's sperm, artificial insemination with donor sperm, artificial insemination with egg and sperm donors using a surrogate mother, *in vitro* fertilization (IVF) using the egg and sperm of the parents, IVF with Intra-cytoplasmic sperm injection (ICSI), IVF with frozen embryos, IVF with pre-implantation genetic diagnosis (PGD), IVF with an egg donor, IVF with a sperm donor, IVF with an egg and sperm donor, IVF with surrogate mother using the parents' egg and sperm, IVF with a surrogate and egg donor, IVF with a surrogate and sperm donor, IVF with a surrogate using her own egg and sperm from the baby's father, IVF with a surrogate using egg and sperm donors, cytoplasmic transfer, and nuclear transfer/cloning.

Gadzooks! OK, I don't know what the word "gadzooks" means any more than I understand many of the listed baby-making techniques. Some pose serious ethical questions and none is 100 percent guaranteed to produce a baby in nine months.

And really now—seventeen additional ways to make a baby? *Whatever happened to the simple "Adam lay with his wife Eve, and she became pregnant" method?* The Lord God created that technique.

What am I doing wrong? I wondered.

I went through a time when I would've endured any pain and would've paid any amount of money to have a baby. Take it from me: these decisions must be made with a clear mind and a prayerful heart.

Even through the confusing maze of infertility, God promises to instruct.

Show me the way, Lord. Show me the way.

Bearing Fruit

Consider prayerfully and study carefully before taking any steps in the quest of fertility. Absolutely, positively, do not rush into any technique without the full understanding of what it entails financially and ethically. Remember, there is no 100 percent guarantee of success with any of them, and ultimately all conception requires the hand of God.

Day Four

The "Murky Mire" of Romans, Chapter Seven

"I do not understand what I do. For what I want to do I do not do, but what I hate I do...For I have the desire to do what is good, but I cannot carry it out. For what I do is not the good I want to do; no, the evil I do not want to do— this I keep on doing. When I want to do good, evil is right there with me. What a wretched man I am! Who will rescue me from this body of death? Thanks be to God—through Jesus Christ our Lord."

—Romans 7:15,18–19, 21, 24–25

Didn't do it. Didn't turn to the Spirit. Didn't turn to His strength. Didn't focus on His Presence and joy. Didn't do it.

I allowed a mean, dark, festering attitude to grow in my heart until it overtook and emerged as a raging, foul, and foolish, furious beast. It was about *choice* and I chose to allow weakness to rule. It was about choice and I chose to allow failure to reign.

Why do I rage against God's Spirit? Why is it so easy to fall back on those ungodly ways? It is because I am flesh. Because I get so caught up in the murky mire of Romans, Chapter Seven.

In the shattering of my dream of motherhood I have seen many ugly sins rise to the surface—jealousy, anger, depression, selfishness.

But, thankfully—Christ rescues me from myself!

And when I come to my spiritual senses, I run to the Lord, confessing the sin. Forgiveness calms my heart. Then He empowers me to do His work.

No matter how dirty I am, He fully cleanses me.

Bearing Fruit

Confess quickly when you are in a Romans, Chapter Seven, struggle—your spirit warring against your fleshly desire. Infertility stirs up sin frequently and easily. So just confess it and get clean.

Day Five

An Onslaught of Negative Emotions

"Now we know that if the earthly tent we live in is destroyed, we have a building from God, an eternal house in heaven, not built by human hands. Meanwhile, we groan, longing to be clothed with our heavenly dwelling, because when we are clothed, we will not be found naked. For while we are in this tent, we groan and are burdened, because we do not wish to be unclothed but to be clothed with our heavenly dwelling, so that what is mortal may be swallowed up by life."

—2 Corinthians 5:1–4

I don't know how to fight these feelings. When I think of not being able to have children, I feel hurt and angry. I hate the jealousy. I hate the self-focus. I hate the anger. I hate the depression.

I groan, crushed by the onslaught of the negative emotions that are constantly attacking my heart.

I want to ask for help; I keep asking God for help. I keep telling my soul to be calm, to *be quiet*. I am afraid to appear weak. I want to be strong. I want to be back at the business of life. I don't know how to appropriately feel sadness. I'm angry that someone doesn't have a magic wand to wave that would make it all better. I don't know how to ask for love and help without feeling intrusive.

I want to break out of my skin!

Bearing Fruit

While you live in this earthly tent, you'll experience sinful and selfish emotions. There will be days when you won't know where to turn or how to pull yourself out of such negative feelings. If possible, take some time to be alone on those days. Have a good cry session. As my friend puts it, "Go to the wailing wall." Let God comfort you. He will…just as He promises.

Day Six

Profitable in Pain

"Rejoice that you participate in the sufferings of Christ, so that you may be overjoyed when his glory is revealed. Those who suffer according to God's will should commit themselves to their faithful Creator and continue to do good."

—I Peter 4:13, 19

Be profitable in pain. This is what God asks of me. This is the state of motion for which to strive when engulfed in pain. I am not to be paralyzed by the pain, but am to continue through it. Despite the pain of childlessness, I am still to serve others and strive to ease their pain.

At times I feel paralyzed by the realization that I may forever be childless. But I have a friend who is in a wheelchair—and who often, usually unknowingly—teaches me great truths. She has cerebral palsy, and even the task of lifting a fork to her mouth is difficult, yet she does it. She is very *profitable in her pain.* She does not allow the pain and struggle to stop her. She is dynamic, a constant blur of motion, and a consistent vessel, greatly used of God. All of this profitable activity takes place despite her "disability."

My disability is hidden. And the symptoms affect my emotions more than my physical ability. I sometimes feel hindered by infertility. I often want to just hide away and not face life. Then I see my friend zipping around in her wheelchair. Her dogged determination to carry out the Lord's work sparks a fire within me. I'm awakened from my paralyzed state.

So I am determined to be profitable in my pain of infertility. I will continue to be an obedient servant to the Lord. I hate being here, drenched in difficult circumstances, but I refuse to let it paralyze my ability to do good.

Bearing Fruit

Do you know someone with a physical disability? Learn from them if they carry on courageously. Read a Joni Eareckson Tada book. Heaven: Your Real Home *is one of my favorites. We need never be limited spiritually by a physical disability.*

Day Seven

Judging Justice

"'I hate divorce,' says the Lord God of Israel, 'and I hate a man's covering himself with violence, as with his garment,' says the Lord Almighty. So guard yourself in your spirit, and do not break faith."

—*Malachi 2:16*

Deep within me bubbled a hot, rising volcanic lava flow of anger at the injustice of it. An acquaintance had finally gotten pregnant. The rage that festered within me was because her marriage was in shambles, the couple on the verge of divorce. This attempt at pregnancy seemed nothing short of a *last ditch effort* to keep her husband, if you asked me.

It made absolutely no sense to my finite mind and broken heart that the Lord would grant them a child in the midst of a volatile situation. Her husband had no intention of staying with her or of salvaging the marriage—baby or no baby. Regardless of the beautiful baby they soon had, they split up, after which a messy custody battle was fought.

While my husband and I don't have a perfect marriage, it *is* a stable one, and we are committed to staying together. A child would have a stable and loving home here with us. *So*—I pondered—*where is God's sense of social services? Why had the Judge placed a child in a broken home and not in our stable home?*

As I wept and prayed over this puzzling situation, God, the Father, revealed to me His own deep feelings regarding this scenario: "I hate divorce," His Word said. God also revealed to me that I am not to judge the validity of a life being given by Him, where that child should live, or who that child's parents should be. I am not even to judge the actions of those parents.

God, the Father, understands parenthood. In fact, He created it.

My anger subsided and instead I prayed for that broken home and the child that God had placed there.

Bearing Fruit

Pray for children of broken homes. Be a compassionate friend to someone whose marriage is in trouble.

Day Eight

Spirit Interpretation

"In the same way, the Spirit helps us in our weakness. We do not know what we ought to pray for, but the Spirit himself intercedes for us with groans that words cannot express. And he who searches our hearts knows the mind of the Spirit, because the Spirit intercedes for the saints in accordance with God's will."

—Romans 8:26–27

My thoughts fly to heaven, lifted by the Holy Spirit. Though they are jumbled and confused by the distress in my heart, the Holy Spirit makes sense of them. Many prayers have come in deep groans of heaviness over my inability to become a mother.

Only the childless understand this pain. It perpetually lingers at the edge of my consciousness. I am constantly aware on some level that I am missing something, someone. I can only file this *missing person report* to God. Just as a police officer makes sense of and brings clarity to the words of a distraught crime victim, the Spirit reveals my deepest hurt to the Father. The Spirit essentially files the report with Him.

And I can rest secure knowing that a Just and Righteous Lord has heard my plea and is taking action in my heart.

Bearing Fruit

Much of the pain we feel over our childlessness is too deep for words. Groans are all we have. It is helpful and healing to journal your thoughts, feelings, and prayers. This helped me tremendously. In fact, you're getting a peek at some of my journal today. . . .

Day Nine

Pray Like Hannah

"In bitterness of soul, Hannah wept much and prayed to the Lord."

—I Samuel 1:10

"God loves to be pursued," Annie Chapman once said. "Hannah confronted God about her barrenness. I admire a woman who will do battle with God like Hannah did. Hannah wanted to hear God's Voice for herself. He responded, and she came away with a heart at peace."

Pursue God passionately with prayer was the message.

I must do this with the same amount of energy as I use to weep over my childlessness. God certainly doesn't cower at my confrontation. He sees my heart and its honest pain. He knows I trust Him, but He allows me to grieve freely.

I must pursue the Lord with the courage of Hannah. She understood the sovereignty of the Lord Almighty and cried out for His mercy.

I, too, have wept those same bitter tears. I, too, have pleaded for a child. God has not granted my "Samuel," but He has granted me peace. Hannah had peace as she wiped the tears from her face.

I passionately love the Lord and passionately trust in His sovereignty.

Bearing Fruit

Hannah's Prayer Ministries can be found on the Internet at www.hannah.org. This is a site for sore eyes— eyes weary from the tears of infertility.

Day Ten

Insensitivity from a Fellow Infertile

*"Take up the shield of faith,
with which you can extinguish all the flaming
arrows of the evil one."*

—Ephesians 6:16

A mother who had been infertile for many years told me the story of her "miracle child." It was a pleasant enough story, though I had heard so many of them before. Yet this story suddenly took a twist that blindsided me when she spoke haughtily.

"The difference between *us* is that I always knew I had the promise of a child. I don't think you have that. In you, I see despair."

Excuse me? What did you just say?

I never expected an insensitive remark from someone who had known the struggle of infertility. But there it was, piercing me clean through to my heart. God gave me the grace not to rip her face off! But when the shock of her comments wore off, the pain was deep.

It's sad, but insensitive and inappropriate comments can come crashing in from *anyone,* anywhere, anytime. There are many who think they have the market cornered on knowing God's will and they are ever-ready to enlighten you with "supernatural wisdom." When this happens, you'd be well-advised to recognize the actual source of their "truth— the father of lies.

Even in suffering we must be battle-ready, holding high the shield of faith to ward off Satan's volley of fire.

Bearing Fruit

Now, this was a real shocker to me—Insensitive comments from someone who knew the same pain I lived with daily. Be ready for anything!

Day Eleven

Discipline

"For God did not give us a spirit of timidity, but a spirit of power, of love, and of self–discipline."

—2 Timothy 1:7

When did I lose the courage to stick with something despite difficulties? Part of it can be attributed to the lessons ingrained in me by my culture. My whole view of how things should be is microwave-oriented. Better, faster, *now*!

Much of the problem stems from a lack of discipline. Discipline is seen as drudgery and I sometimes too quickly abandon it and move on to an expedient way of doing things.

God supplies the power for discipline. While pursuing a disciplined life I may feel like it's drudgery, but there is a higher purpose. I like what Oswald Chambers writes regarding patience and discipline:

> [God] is never in a hurry. Yet we are always in such a frantic hurry. God has to take us into the valley and put us through fires and floods to batter us into shape.

So, I must slow down. I must brace up and face the valley of difficulties. I won't run from adversity. And I won't timidly cower from this monster of infertility.

Bearing Fruit

Power, love, and self-discipline. God supplies it all. You will need all of these in facing this monster. Pray hard for these attributes.

Day Twelve

In Step with the Spirit

"The acts of the sinful nature are obvious: hatred, discord, jealousy, fits of rage, selfish ambition, dissensions, factions and envy and the like. I warn you, as I did before, that those who live like this will not inherit the kingdom of God. But the fruit of the Spirit is love, joy, peace, patience, kindness, goodness, faithfulness, gentleness and self-control. Against such things there is no law. Those who belong to Christ Jesus have crucified the sinful nature with its passions and desires. Since we live by the Spirit, let us keep in step with the Spirit."

—Galatians 5:19–25

At times the flesh calls to me, daring me to move closer to the treacherous twister of temptation. But through Jesus I can get a grip. I can stop the whirlwind of temptation by holding on to the Cross. The Cross is the only stability, the only escape from the sin of my flesh, because my sin was paid for and defeated by Jesus' sacrifice. Galatians 5:24–25 is a great promise and a true encouragement.

I tend to focus on the fruit-of-the-Spirit verses found in Galatians 5:22–23. Those verses are sandwiched by the acts of the sinful nature and the Crucifixion of the sinful nature and living by the Spirit, keeping in step with the Spirit.

I choose to make this day far different from yesterday. I cannot change yesterday's sinful acts, but today is mine. This moment is mine, and the next and the next and the next.

I choose to keep in step with the Spirit.

Bearing Fruit

Memorize each aspect of the fruit of the Spirit (love, joy, peace, patience, kindness, goodness, faithfulness, gentleness and self-control). When you are tempted to engage in self-pity or to sin because of your childlessness, ask the Spirit's help to exhibit one of the seven fruits.

Day Thirteen

Simple Math

"[You] made the Lord angry.... You did not trust or obey Him."

—Deuteronomy 9:22, 23

It all comes down to a simple mathematical equation: "Trust + Obedience = Peace."

Struggling so hard against my circumstances is futile. They do not budge. They will not relent. I cannot change the fact that we have been unable to bear children. But my sustained anger against this fact tarnishes my trust in God.

As trust diminishes, my obedience is corroded. This only serves to taint my heart with unrest and discontentment.

My rebellion against the Lord's will for me at present gains nothing for me but His discipline. I become soaked with the sweat of my obstinacy, fatigued by my fears. It is displeasing to my Father.

It takes a continual mathematical drill of discipline to remind myself: "Trust + Obedience = Peace."

Bearing Fruit

Anger is a part of infertility. A sustained anger that you allow to fester and grow, however, becomes rebellion. You will know when it reaches a dangerous stage by the constant churning of your heart; when it seems nothing can give you peace. Only by reaffirming your trust in the Lord will you find peace. That takes prayer—constant, steadfast, and disciplined prayer. Talk to God about your anger today. King David did, and God's big enough to take it.

Day Fourteen

A Pure Heart

"Create in me a pure heart, O God, and renew a steadfast spirit within me. Do not cast me from your presence or take your Holy Spirit from me. Restore to me the joy of your salvation and grant me a willing spirit to sustain me."

—Psalm 51:10–12

My heart is the source of love and the source of selfishness. From it, God's love encourages others and from it my judgment cuts them down. From it, God's compassion overflows to comfort another, and from it I churn with jealousy and disappointment and reject others.

It is easy to get so caught up in the pain of my infertility that my heart sometimes becomes hard against the needs of others. I must soften my selfish heart with the Word of God. When I am filled with the joy of His salvation, my wicked heart is purified.

The Holy Spirit fills my spirit with an energizing sustenance. He takes my eyes off "poor me," guiding and directing my heart to care for others. Then my heart exudes His love and compassion—His perfect comfort. *May God create in me a clean, pure heart!*

Bearing Fruit

Examine your heart. Ask the Lord to diagnose your "heart condition." If there is any hardness in your heart, go to God's Word for softening. You will offset the pain of infertility with the joy found in His Word.

Day Fifteen

Dry and Weary, Barren Land

"O God, you are my God, earnestly I seek you;
my soul thirsts for you,
my body longs for you, in a dry and weary land."

—Psalm 63:1

Life is a whirlwind. I hardly seem conscious of breathing, let alone all the other tasks that clamor to be noticed. Only one task I desire— to seek hard after God. But many things beg for my attention.

On the roller coaster ride of fertility success, I find it difficult indeed to focus. My life seems like one long fertility checklist: 1) Call doctor, 2) go to appointment, 3) pick up prescription, 4) take fertility medication, 5) take temperature, 6) chart ovulation progress, 7) check for ovulation, 8) have intercourse, 9) wait, wait, wait, wait, wait, wait for a sign of menstruation, 10) cry, 11) call doctor.

In the dry and weary, barren land of infertility, as the sandstorms of medical efforts whirl around me, may I pause and lift my soul to God and drink from His satisfying, living water!

Bearing Fruit

It is an arduous and endless cycle when you are making a concentrated effort to get pregnant. Take a few months off from it now and then. Go on a weekend getaway and enjoy the romance of intimacy instead of viewing it as just a means to an end. Get off the ferris wheel of infertility and get back on stable ground.

Day Sixteen

Pouring My Heart Out

"I call with all my heart; answer me, O Lord, and I will obey your decrees.
I call out to you; save me and I will keep your statutes.
Hear my voice in accordance with your love. You are near, O Lord."

—Psalm 119:145–146, 149, 151

Complaining vs. "pouring your heart out." *Is there a difference?*

Did David complain? Or did he pour his heart out to God?

The Psalms are a collection of proper complaint methods. If we imagine David praying or singing these songs, we don't hear whininess in them. Rather, we hear from a man who was not afraid to bear his heart before God. He wasn't afraid to be vulnerable in front of the Lord.

This is a lesson from a man who knew how to trust God. David knew *exactly* how to get his complaints resolved. He shows us a genuine and close relationship with the Heavenly Father.

The Psalms mention the *heart* one hundred twenty-eight times.

David's heart beat with the same rhythm as God's.

I will not hide my heart from God. He can plainly see the pain of childlessness. He sees the scar it leaves upon my heart. Still, like David, I will pour out my heart to God. And like David, God will answer me—with all His Heart.

Bearing Fruit

Share your pain with others, but share the worst of it with God. Let all the bitterness seep out. Let all the anger explode. Rid yourself of these poisonous emotions and let God clean up the hazardous waste.

Day Seventeen

Grieving the Holy Spirit

"And do not grieve the Holy Spirit of God, with whom you were sealed for the day of redemption. Get rid of all bitterness, rage, and anger."

—Ephesians 4:30–31

Sometimes I have an "infertility attack." This is when I am struggling desperately with God over the unfairness of my infertility. I am angry, disgusted, and vehemently questioning His will.

During one of these "attacks," my friend patiently went to lunch with me, despite my melancholy and impossible mood. In the course of the conversation, I told her I wasn't talking to God right now. I likened it to the rebellious teenager slamming the bedroom door and cranking up the rock music in protest of parental "unfairness." My friend in her profoundly simple wisdom asked a simple question.

"Where does the Holy Spirit go when you're angry and not talking to God?"

Ummm…

Is that what it means to grieve the Holy Spirit?

As a believer, I know that the Holy Spirit has taken up permanent residence in my spirit. When I am bitter and angry towards God, I am causing the Spirit to grieve. Certainly it is acceptable to be angry and confused by circumstances, but I cannot close myself off from talking to God about these feelings. I *must* take them to Him, with the Spirit interpreting for me. Only then will these deadly feelings be resolved.

Bearing Fruit

What would I do without the accountability of my friend and the stability of the Holy Spirit? You need the wisdom of both in your life.

Day Eighteen

Big Storm in a Little Boat

"A furious squall came up, and the waves broke over the boat, so that it was nearly swamped. Jesus was in the stern, sleeping on a cushion. The disciples woke him and said to him, 'Teacher, don't you care if we drown?' He got up, rebuked the wind and said to the waves, 'Quiet! Be still!' Then the wind died down and it was completely calm."

—Mark 4:37–39

What a whirlwind of a day! I had no inkling that the specialist would advise that we do an insemination the next day.

Ow! Fertility whiplash!

I feel numb. I feel pain in every inch of my universe. *No corner is safe. I want to scream. I want to withdraw. Outside, I laugh, but I want to cry.* I want a child more than anything; yet, at times, the last thing I want is a child. Often I don't know what I want.

Sinking in a quagmire. It continues to be a maze of emotions, a maze of decisions. Like the disciples, tossed about in a little boat in a big storm, I frantically call out to Jesus to save me!

Will my soul ever have quiet peace? My attempts at gaining peace seem to be failing in the face of my prayer. The Lord gently chides me, reminding me that my eternity is secure in Him. I need only to trust and to look to things above, that I might have peace, not for my good, but for God's glory.

I long for peace. I long for the Lord to command the wind and the waves of my circumstances to be still.

Bearing Fruit

Find a hideaway in your home where it is completely quiet. Ask the Lord to still your thoughts. Read from the Psalms for comfort. Listen to worship music. Close your eyes and let His peace sweep over you. Relax. Be quiet. Be still.

Day Nineteen

A Constant Twinge

"To keep me from becoming conceited, there was given me a thorn in my flesh, a messenger of Satan to torment me."

—2 Corinthians 12:7

Seems rather harsh that I must go through life being reminded at every turn of what I am missing. I am surrounded by taunts of my inadequacy, my "curse," and my "cross to bear" —a constant twinge caused by this thorn in my flesh. Babies and children everywhere, announcements of pregnancies, baby shower invitations, and baby dedications at church.... The fruitful propagation of the planet scoffs at my barren womb.

As He did with Paul, did the Lord send this *strange messenger* to keep me from being arrogant? *I must consider my heart carefully to see if there is any prideful, wicked way in me.*

All in all, as with Paul: God's grace *can* be sufficient for all things. The question is: *Will I allow it to be?*

When faced with a steady flow of pain, will I allow His grace to satisfy me?

Bearing Fruit

You never get away from reminders of your childlessness. Infertility is not a consequence for sin (unless you did something to harm yourself), but it can reveal sin. Maybe you thought you had it all, and now this is something you can't attain. You may be responding in a sinful way. Examine your heart. Confess any wrongdoing in order to get clean of impurities. And when the images of fertility taunt you, allow His grace to satisfy.

Day Twenty

Hannah's Rival

"And because the Lord had closed her womb, her rival kept provoking her in order to irritate her. This went on year after year. Whenever Hannah went up to the house of the Lord, her rival provoked her till she wept and would not eat. In bitterness of soul Hannah wept much and prayed to the Lord."

—I Samuel 1:6–7, 10

Infertility infiltrates every corner of life. There is no escape from its relentless pursuit. I am constantly reminded of my inadequacy, my inability to achieve a goal, a seemingly simple, commonplace goal. I can't even accomplish what I was created and designed to do.

This spills over into every other area. My career, my role as a wife and as a friend, my ministry, everything is seen as *lacking*, as if somehow everything is my fault. *I feel like a failure. A big loser. A varsity loser.*

I guess I feel like Hannah may have felt, constantly provoked by her rival Peninnah, who gloated in her own fertility and scoffed at Hannah's infertility. Satan is my worst rival, telling me I am nothing because I am barren. Why do I allow myself to get caught up in his lies?

Hannah exemplifies what I must do. Lay it out before the Lord. Lay my embittered soul before Him and vow to trust. And pray and pray and pray.

He may not promise everyone a child, but He does promise peace to those who seek it.

Bearing Fruit

You'll never escape it—constant reminders of your infertility are everywhere. And its poison leaks into every aspect of your life. It will sully your soul. Read Empty Womb, Aching Heart *by Marlo Schalesky. In it, you will find fellow Hannahs and Elkanahs sharing their stories. Peace will come as you glean comfort from their words.*

Day Twenty-One

I May Never Be a Mom

"Why are you downcast, O my soul? Why so disturbed within me?
Put your hope in God, for I will yet praise Him, my Savior and my God."

—*Psalm 42:11*

Taking a dunk into depression. *I hate this. No matter what anyone says or does, it doesn't seem to lift me up. I don't want to feel this way. I am allowing myself to believe Satan's lies—listening to that whisper, that constant and relentless whisper.* Even when I am fully aware that it's a lie, I allow myself the luxury to wallow in self-pity and believe I'm never going to feel good again.

My mind races at a feverish pitch. *Why can't I quiet my soul? I shush it, but it shouts all the louder.*

Last week I couldn't even say or write the following: "I may never be a mom." Even now, looking at it strikes deep. *How will I ever come to terms with it? I feel heavyhearted. I will allow myself some time to grieve.*

"I may never be a mom." I try to say that over and over until a peaceful heart, content in the sovereignty of God, enables me to say those words.

"I may never be a mom."

Today, I can't get it out without a wobble in my throat. My weary soul repeats the sad refrain.

"I may never be a mom. But, I place all my hope in God and praise Him—my Savior and my God!"

My soul is lifted.

Bearing Fruit

When reality hits, respond accordingly. Allow yourself to be sad, but then allow God to lift you up. This may come in any number of ways: through the love of your husband, a friend, an encouraging note, or in reading God's Word. Allow His promises to lift up your downcast soul.

PART TWO

Modified Relationships: What Changes Occur With Others

"Infertility puts pressure on individuals and marriages.
Marriage must be top priority during infertility.
If we're never able to have our dream children,
we'll still have a soul mate, and the strong,
supportive relationship we've cultivated."

— Debra Bridwell,
from *The Ache for a Child*

"A new command I give you: Love one another. As I have loved you, so you must love one another."

—John 13:34

Any crisis or circumstance changes relationships, but infertility touches *every* relationship, including spouse, family, friends, coworkers, neighbors—basically everyone in your sphere of contact. Even casual conversations…with their generic questions about marriage, children, etc., … bring awkward moments.

While there are countless negatives involved, infertility can also reveal true bonding among those who will tough it out with you.

Day Twenty-Two

The "Big-O" Week

"Listen! My lover! Look! Here he comes, leaping across the mountains, bounding over the hills. My lover is like a gazelle or a young stag. Look! There he stands behind our wall, gazing through the windows, peering through the lattice. My lover spoke and said to me, 'Arise, my darling, my beautiful one, and come with me.'"

—*Song of Songs 2:8–10*

My anger seethed at my husband. He sometimes gave lame answers about why he didn't want to have intercourse during ovulation week. *What was he thinking?* I thought we both really wanted a baby.

Not only was I gaining weight due to the fertility drugs, but my emotions were haywire as well (thanks also to the fertility drugs). When my husband would not cooperate during "The Big-O Week," it seemed like a waste of our money, our efforts, my body, and my sanity.

During these times, clear communication was desperately needed. It didn't help matters that I was a mass of raging hormones, distressed about my flabby body and depressed that we had to go to such lengths for a child.

Honestly, my husband and I never did learn how to communicate effectively during these times. But I believe it is essential for a couple to work at this.

I also realized that if we didn't have intercourse on a particular night during the "Big-O Week," God was not slapping His Almighty Forehead in frustration saying, "Oh great! *This* was the night they would've conceived their child. Now what do I do?"

If it's going to happen, it's going to happen. Your job is to keep up the pursuit, but back off if it gets to be too much. And yes, it sometimes will!

Bearing Fruit

Funny how the very act that is necessary to having a child is often what suffers the most in the process. It won't always be romantic during the "Big-O Week," but it does no good to get flustered if once in a while your spouse is not all that interested. Chill out, take a deep breath, and just give a little kiss of understanding. And hey, you never know where that little kiss may lead.

Day Twenty-Three

Stability in a Shaky Marriage

"Love and faithfulness meet together; righteousness and peace kiss each other."

—*Psalm 85:10*

When we repent of sin, the Lord's blessings are like kisses that take away the sting of guilt. There have been many painful arguments with my husband that were infertility-fueled. I have sinned many times over with the hateful words I've spewed at the dearest, sweetest man a woman could ever want. He has been an easy target to alleviate the frustrations I have with my barren womb. We have both sometimes blamed each other for our inability to conceive.

The Lord, our Rock, has been the stability for our shaky marriage.

Infertility can easily break up a marriage, but God has used it to strengthen ours. We had to make the choice: we chose repentance. And as a result, we have grown closer through this strange and sad journey. The Lord has shown such love.

Yes, the Lord's blessings are kisses indeed.

Bearing Fruit

If you are having marriage difficulties due to infertility, don't let them fester. The difficulties will come, but clear communication and forgiveness are needed to relieve the stress. Get counseling if needed. You're already faced with the potential loss of being a parent; don't compound it with the loss of your marital relationship.

Day Twenty-Four

Filling Empty Arms

"Two are better than one, if one falls down, his friend can help him up.
Also, if two lie down together, they will keep warm.
A cord of three strands is not quickly broken."

—Ecclesiastes 4:9–12

I wish that I could give you a son.

A little boy who would grow up wanting to be just like his Daddy—

A son who would watch every step his father took and shadow each one,

A young man who would say his hero was his Dad,

A man with his father's handsome smile and courageous heart,

Oh, how I long to give you a son!

I wish that I could give you a daughter.

A little girl who would grow up wanting to marry someone just like her Daddy—

A daughter who would run to her father's arms and cover him with kisses,

A young woman who would say her hero was her Dad,

A woman with her father's eyes and compassionate heart,

Oh, how I long to give you a daughter!

But wishes and longings and even prayers cannot seem to produce a child—

My body is deficient.

My womb is closed. Barren. Unable to conceive.

I'm so sorry for that. But it's out of my hands.

And I have to believe God is still holy, still sovereign, still trustworthy.

Oh, how I wish I could give you our child—

To fill that need.

To fill your empty arms with our baby.

But, here I stand, with my deficient body. My arms are empty, too.

Perhaps God intends that. So for now, we fill them with each other.

Bearing Fruit

Share with your husband the pain you feel over missing out on his fatherhood. Tell him how much you love him. Appreciate the man he is. Kneel together before the Lord and ask Him to bless your love and give you the strength to hold each other up through these difficult times.

Day Twenty-Five

My Husband's Depression

*"Let us rejoice and be glad and give him glory!
For the wedding of the Lamb has come,
and his bride has made herself ready. The Spirit
and the bride say,
'Come!' Amen. Come, Lord Jesus."*

—Revelation 19:7; 22:17, 20

I took for granted that my emotions were much deeper than my husband's in this infertility mess. And then *he* became depressed.

Personalitywise, I am sanguine and my husband is melancholy. So I shouldn't have been surprised at the depth of his depression when it hit. He'd faced a major disappointment at work. I was scheduled for surgery to correct some female problems, and it had been a long road of struggle with infertility.

The depression hit Ed hard. And it imprisoned his heart for a long time.

There was nothing I could do for him. He was angry with God. He was so angry he even stopped attending church. He wouldn't discuss it with anyone. He just brooded and sank deeper and deeper into the pit of despair.

It was so intense and prolonged that it almost drove me away. I was so angry with him. I was the one facing surgery, and I needed his support. But that didn't faze him. Depression does that. You are numb to everyone else's feelings.

His anger with God grew. Thankfully, I had support in other areas of my life and much prayer was going out for us. So I stayed. I stayed with a man I didn't recognize.

My surgery pulled him out of the pit.

He shared with me later that watching me go through the surgery brought him to his senses. As he slowly began to pray again, he said, he realized that part of his difficulty was anger at God over not getting his way. He couldn't change the status of things by making demands of God. Depression loosened its grip as he reached for the Sovereign Lord.

This was a turning point in our marriage. We both realized how much we loved each other, how much we were committed to stay with each other no matter what. As I put it, "We finally found each other."

Without the holy example of unconditional love that God had shown us, even to the point of the Lord Jesus dying on the Cross, we would not have known that it takes *sacrifice* to love. Without the forgiveness of sins that came through the Lord's death on the Cross we wouldn't have forgiven each other. And without the glorious Resurrection and the promise that He will someday come for His Bride, we would never have known how to love so powerfully. Without the holy example of our Lord, the Bridegroom, we would not have known how to love each other so completely.

After almost thirteen years of marriage it is amazing to me to find the most profound expression of Christ's love revealed in the loving eyes of my husband.

Bearing Fruit

Don't forget your husband's emotions in this. Regardless of how it comes across, your husband is bound to experience some sadness over his childlessness. Stick by him if he goes through a particularly difficult time. Let him have his time of grief. He will probably go through it differently than you do. Just pray him through it. If depression hangs on for months at a time for either of you, seek counseling. A deeper pit of depression calls for more helping hands.

Day Twenty-Six

A Touch from God

"In all our distress and persecution we were encouraged...because of your faith. How can we thank God enough for you in return for all the joy we have in the presence of our God because of you? May God himself, the God of peace, sanctify you through and through."

—I Thessalonians 3:7, 9; 5:23

It marked a turning point in a friendship, as well as in my infertility journey.

I had been sharing my infertility struggles with a friend at work. One morning I checked my email and one of the first messages I read was from this friend. She had sent it to all the staff and it read simply: "I'm going to be a grandma!"

My heart fell. I felt my anger rise. I wondered how she, of all people, could do something as insensitive as sending this email to me. She knew how I was struggling. I was shocked and disappointed in her. *Why didn't she break the news to me gently?* I could've easily allowed myself to wall up my heart from her, run away angry, refusing to trust her anymore with my pain. But instead we confronted it.

I revealed my anger and hurt and took the risk of being vulnerable. I listened to her side of it. She said she travailed over whether to include me in the email or not. But she decided she wasn't going to isolate me as if I were some different creature. She told me that when her daughter announced the pregnancy she was so ecstatic for her daughter, but her thoughts also went to my pain. She cried, she got down on her knees and took my hand. I sensed such love and compassion from her; it overwhelmed me.

Suddenly, it became clear to me that this was a touch from God.

He, too, hurts for me—travails for me. His thoughts fly to my pain. He is not insensitive and uncaring. He had not forgotten me in my infertility struggle. I guess at times I wanted to run from Him, angry, not wanting to trust anymore. But that day was a turning point. God had not abandoned me in my infertility.

That friend became my best friend—and the one who has been most instrumental in my healing.

Bearing Fruit

Avoid jumping to conclusions when you feel you've been wronged. Instead, confront in love. You may discover a best friend because of it. I did.

Day Twenty-Seven

Blessings from Obedience

"As Jesus was saying these things, a woman in the crowd called out, 'Blessed is the mother who gave you birth and nursed you.' He replied, 'Blessed rather are those who hear the word of God and obey it.'"

—Luke 11:27–28

My friend's daughter was pregnant. My friend had wept with me when I wept over my infertility; now it was my turn to rejoice with her as she rejoiced. She was sensitive to me…and without excluding me from the joyous unfolding of the pregnancy.

At first through gritted teeth and a forced smile, I would dutifully ask how the pregnancy was going. But I asked, and I sincerely wanted to share in the joy.

As the delivery date drew closer, her daughter began having some difficulty. I prayed with fervency. With each prayer it became easier to focus on mother and child, and I found myself thinking less of my own pain. Soon I was celebrating the arrival of a baby girl.

My friend observed that she sensed a new freedom in me as I gradually relaxed and accepted the pregnancy. She considered this a blessing from God and attributed it to my obedience to prayer and my determination to be happy for others, despite my own pain.

My infertility should not shut down my compassion for others. It especially should not shut down my ability to intercede for those whom God has placed in my life.

Selfishness slowly turns into selflessness as I spend time in prayer. I find that my heart cannot be jealous of someone I am lifting before the throne of God.

Bearing Fruit

Faithfully pray for those close to you who are pregnant. It's good for them and, believe it or not, it's good for you. God blesses obedience.

Day Twenty-Eight

Extreme Relationships

"If anyone comes to me and does not hate his father and mother, his wife and children, his brothers and sisters—yes, even his own life—he cannot be my disciple."

—Luke 14:26

Barb and Doug, mission leaders in Haiti, said this during a short-term missions trip, circa January, 1990: "Let go of everything, because having Him and being in His perfect will is more precious than *any* human relationship or treasure."

Their words touched me deeply and reminded me of a truth I knew but had never applied to my situation. We are to put no human relationship above our Lord. It threw my spiritual understanding into a tailspin when the Holy Spirit impressed upon me that this included even my "dream child," who is nonexistent at this point. I could easily focus my energies exclusively on the quest of that little one…devote my whole heart to the dream of a little love.

In putting my dream baby first, in the words of Oswald Chambers, I "cannot be someone over whom Jesus can write the word 'mine.' Any one of the relationships our Lord mentions in this verse

[Luke 14:26] can compete with our relationship with Him."

Jesus taught using an extreme comparison. In order to be His disciple we must supremely love Him, to the extent of seeming to *hate* all others by comparison.

No relationship should be above my relationship with Jesus. In the past I have found myself obsessing over the child I do not have. This has hindered my intimacy with the Lord on many levels and in many facets.

Jesus is the joy of my heart. My desire is to look at Him and at all that He has given, not to what I *wish* I had.

Bearing Fruit

Are you putting your "dream child" above Jesus? If so, you are missing out on His discipleship. Reevaluate and recommit to Him.

Day Twenty-Nine

Just Be There

"I have heard many things like these; miserable comforters are you all! Will your longwinded speeches never end? What ails you that you keep on arguing? I could also speak like you, if you were in my place; I could make fine speeches against you and shake my head at you."

—Job 16:1–4

Not only did Job struggle with the suffering of his losses. He also had to contend with friends who did little to comfort him. I can surely relate to Job in this way. I am often confronted by the insensitive remarks of others about my infertility. Sometimes even those who care about me have made comments that only burdened me more.

Job's friends had it right at first. When they first came on the scene they just sat with Job, not saying anything. But when people suffer, we want to help them. Silence can be awkward, but it's best not to fill the silence with unwanted advice or empty platitudes.

I learned this invaluable lesson some years ago when my friend had a miscarriage. I went over to her house one evening. We watched an old movie, ate popcorn, conversed a bit, and laughed a little. The subject of her miscarriage never came up. When I was getting ready to leave, we hugged. She held on tightly. She thanked me for being such a comfort to her. Surprised, I responded that I didn't feel I had done much. I'll never forget her words.

"You were here for me. No one else calls or comes around. They don't know what to say, so they avoid me altogether. Your presence did more than any words could've done."

I have come to understand and appreciate that lesson.

Resist the urge to say something if you have no words. Acknowledge the pain and just *be there*. That will comfort more than anything.

Bearing Fruit

The next time someone is sharing burdens with you, embrace the silence. Unless asked for advice, offer none. Just be there.

Day Thirty

Let Them Know

"As God's chosen people, holy and dearly loved,
clothe yourselves with compassion,
kindness, humility, gentleness and patience. And
over all these virtues put on love,
which binds them all together in perfect unity."

—Colossians 3:12, 14

Though most everyone at work was sympathetic to my struggle (and I am probably unaware of those who faithfully prayed for me or to what extent they prayed), a few went "above and beyond" in consistently asking me how I was doing. And after inquiring, those few took the time to actually listen. They acknowledged my pain without offering any quick answers or grand platitudes or "infertility success stories." They simply listened, and often their eyes glistened with tears.

I wanted to express my gratitude. I wanted them to know that, though it may have seemed insignificant, the impact of their genuine concern was, in fact, highly significant to me. So, I obtained a little gift for each of them and wrote sentiments of gratitude in cards. I just had to let them know what their kindness had done for my heart.

An expression of gratitude for kindness given shows the love of Christ in an eternally satisfying way.

Bearing Fruit

Show your gratitude for someone who has been especially sympathetic and kind during this struggle. Give them a card or a little gift...or treat them to dinner.

Day Thirty-One

Not Barren of Compassion

"Live in harmony with one another; be sympathetic, love as brothers, be compassionate and humble."

—I Peter 3:8

How did it happen that I, a childless woman, was entrusted by God with the task of comforting a mother whose heart was breaking? It surprised me when she broke down in my office, revealing her emotion as she explained that her son was moving out. Though she was happy for him and knew that it was time to let go, it was still very difficult for her and she simply broke down, nearly sobbing.

Now, somehow, at this moment I was empowered by God to extend compassion to her, to listen to her, to let her unload her burden. We hugged and she thanked me for comforting her, even in the midst of my own struggles.

When she left I marveled at God's strange assignments.

Each of us bears pain that is real. I cannot look at someone and say (or even think), "Well, at least you have children...." My pain of infertility does not exist on some ethereal "level 10" of suffering.

In the matter of heartache, all pain is equal.

I still need to be available and willing to comfort a mother, despite my own painful circumstances.

Infertility need not make me barren of compassion.

Bearing Fruit

Open your heart to the pain of others. Be sympathetic to all—yes, even to mothers. Don't allow Satan to feed you the lie that a mother's pain does not compare to yours. Ask the Lord to pour out His compassion through your touch.

Day Thirty-Two

The Guilt Factor

"What a wretched man I am! Who will rescue me
from this body of death?
Thanks be to God—through Jesus Christ our
Lord!
Therefore there is now no condemnation for those
who are in Christ Jesus,
because through Christ Jesus the law of the Spirit
of life set me free
from the law of sin and death."

—Romans 7:24–25, 8:1–2

The burden of my infertility weighed more heavily upon me because I felt responsible for my husband's childlessness, too. The guilt factor intensified because *I* was the one with "the problem." Sometimes I would see my husband's pain and I'd sink deeper into the muck of guilt, the mire of anguish. I would sink so deeply that I couldn't reach him. Though I longed to comfort him, I could not. I asked for forgiveness, for release from this guilt, but my husband did not hear me, and he did not save me.

Yet I dealt more quickly with my feelings of depression than did he, perhaps because I was the one "afflicted." Later, when I would see my husband's pain, I was riding on the wings of contentment, filled with the peace of God. I was so far above him that

I couldn't reach my husband. Though I longed to comfort him, I could not. I tried to use words and attempted to illuminate a path to where I was, but he could not hear me…and he would not follow.

Only the Lord Jesus could save me from drowning in my guilt and only the Lord Jesus could shine a path for my husband to find his own way to contentment.

Bearing Fruit

Speak openly and honestly with your spouse when discovering that one of you has the medical "problem." You're both infertile, despite specific medical reasons. Bring guilt feelings before the Lord Jesus and let Him dispose of them with the reminder that He is sovereign.

Day Thirty-Three

Welcome to Motherhood

"Who is like the Lord our God, the One who sits enthroned on high,
who stoops down to look on the heavens and the earth?
He settles the barren woman in her home as a happy mother of children. Praise the Lord."

—Psalm 113:5–6, 9

Feeling great frustration and exasperation I asked my friend how it was that I could give her encouragement, yet it would seem not to help her at all. When others said and did the same things I did, sometimes verbatim, she believed their words and found encouragement.

She looked at me and said, "Welcome to motherhood."

She explained that she understood my frustration since she had experienced the same when trying to encourage her kids. She smiled with wisdom and I knew that there was a deeper teaching in this moment.

The Lord frequently gives me opportunities to experience the emotions of motherhood without the benefits of a child. This was just another way for me to live out the ups and downs of being a mother. It was another lesson to remind me that just because someone is a mother doesn't mean she is so much more content and happier than I am.

Life is full of disappointments for everyone, even mothers.

Bearing Fruit

The Lord will provide opportunities for you to experience motherhood. And there will be times you see firsthand some of the negatives of raising children. Remind yourself that there are *negatives rather than idealizing what motherhood must be like.*

Day Thirty-Four

Breaking Down Walls

"If your brother sins against you, go and show him his fault, just between the two of you. If he listens to you, you have won your brother over."

—Matthew 18:15

In the course of my infertility difficulties one of my friends unintentionally made a few comments that stung deeply. She meant no malice, but the words were hurtful, nevertheless. I said nothing to her about these comments, but instead I alienated myself from her. For a few years an uncomfortable wall existed between us.

One day a beautiful flower arrangement was delivered from a group of friends who wanted to let me know they were praying for me. This was at a particularly rough time in the midst of infertility procedures. In an ironic twist I discovered that the friend from whom I had been distancing myself was the one who'd initiated this gesture.

I realized I had to confront her about her past comments. She was mortified to find out she had hurt me. Once we demolished the wall of hurt I could discuss my infertility with her.

I am so thankful for the invaluable lesson I gleaned through that experience.

Most people have the heart to be sensitive and to gratefully receive direction on how to love a friend in a painful time. Instead of building walls of alienation, I am learning to build bridges of honesty and work to educate others about infertility.

Bearing Fruit

Be honest with a family member or friend who unknowingly makes insensitive comments. Don't allow a wall of alienation to get any higher. Most people have no idea what pain their words carry. Gently and lovingly reveal your heart and educate them. It will save a lot of heartache in the long run.

Day Thirty-Five

Wherever You Will Go

"For this is what the Sovereign Lord says: I myself will search for my sheep and look after them. As a shepherd looks after his scattered flock when he is with them, so will I look after my sheep. I will rescue them from all the places where they were scattered on a day of clouds and darkness."

—Ezekiel 34:11–12

The way of infertility is a foreboding valley of unknowns. It is a dark and lonely way. My dear husband is the only other one who walks this particular way, on our particular journey. At times we gain strength from each other, holding one another through the pain.

My husband has been faithful to travel this journey with me through pain, depression, surgeries, disappointments—and he has stayed right with me all the way.

The Lord, our Shepherd, has faithfully led His sheep, despite our proneness to wander from Him. He has been the strength and stamina in our getting through hard times. We might have given up long ago had it not been for the Good Shepherd leading us through the darkest of days.

I have never loved my husband with such intensity and joy and have never felt closer to the Lord Jesus than now as I emerge from the clouds and darkness.

Bearing Fruit

It's vital to find a deeper closeness with your spouse in this time. Don't allow the stress of your quest for a child to mar the growth of your marital relationship. Don't become so obsessed with it that your marriage suffers. There will certainly be ups and downs, but keep looking to the Good Shepherd to guide you, especially when you find yourself drifting away. You and your spouse need each other. Cultivate a bond that will never break. And vow to journey together.

Day Thirty-Six

The Pill

"A cheerful heart is good medicine, but a crushed spirit dries up the bones."

—Proverbs 17:22

One night at a "gathering of gabbing girls," one of my friends related how she was seeing her gynecologist for some female troubles. Part of the treatment meant she would have to go on the birth control pill. She was relating the difficulties she was going through and, in the midst of her monologue, she turned to me and asked, "Are you on *The Pill?*"

There followed about three seconds of dead silence.

Her face slowly turned a crimson shade as she realized what she had just said and to whom she had said it. I slapped my hand on my forehead and groaned.

"Oh, my goodness! So, that's been our problem all these years!" We all burst into a raging fit of laughter, even though my friend was still a bit red.

When the laughter died down, she said to me, "Well, at least I don't first and foremost think of you as infertile."

I smiled at this thought. It was refreshing as I often feel like I wear a scarlet "I" on my forehead as "the cursed Infertile."

Bearing Fruit

Believe it or not, you will find moments of humor in your infertility. Feel free to make jokes when appropriate. It will definitely feel good to laugh and will balance out all those tears you've cried.

Day Thirty-Seven

Say Nothing

"The tongue also is a fire, a world of evil among the parts of the body. It corrupts the whole person, sets the whole course of his life on fire, and is itself set on fire by hell. All kinds of animals, birds, reptiles, and creatures of the sea are being tamed and have been tamed by man, but no man can tame the tongue. It is a restless evil, full of deadly poison."

—James 3:6–8

Who can tame the tongue? Surely not the many who, for lack of anything else, say something insensitive or just plain stupid. Better to say *nothing*. James' wise advice extends far beyond what to say to someone engaged in infertility. When you are unsure what to say to someone in pain, say nothing. Just be there.

I call this list my "Top Ten Things *Not* to Say to a Childless Couple" (and my inner monologue when someone does):

1. "Just relax!" (News flash! Stress doesn't cause infertility; infertility causes stress. And believe me, if there's something medically wrong, no amount of *relaxing* will change it.)

2. "My husband just looks at me and I get pregnant." (Well, that certainly is a major advancement in reproduction.)
3. "I knew someone who adopted and then got pregnant." (Are you saying that we should adopt, then "use" this adopted, "second-rate" child to achieve our ultimate goal of having our own flesh and blood, biological child?

   Or, another variation on this question's theme is: "Have you considered adoption?" If I had a dollar for every time someone asked me that question, I'd have enough money to actually pay for an adoption.)
4. "It must be God's will." (This is a common phrase, used in many circumstances by people who pretty much have no idea what else to say. And although you may have the best intentions at heart, hoping to provide some spiritual encouragement, this question actually has the opposite effect. This is an empty platitude that only burdens me more.)
5. "You can have my kids!" (You know what, I wouldn't *want* your kids.)
6. Macho man says, "Let me have a go at it!" (Hey buddy, one good, swift kick will render you unable to follow through on that.)
7. "Oh, you're much better off without kids anyway." (Now, this one…in the material sense of life, is probably pretty true. I drive a pretty nice car, we have a pretty nice house that's pretty

nice and quiet, with pretty, nice things in it. We can come and go as we please…and yet, if God asked me which I wanted…I'd trade it all for children.)

8. "Have you seen a specialist yet?" (This is similar to the adoption question…and unless you're close to me, that's a rather personal question to ask.)
9. "I knew someone who…. (fill in some surefire technique to get pregnant)." (Look, I really don't want to hear about herbal foods that increase your fertility, or that I should cut out caffeine, or that my husband should wear boxers, or I should put a fertility goddess figurine on our bedpost, etc., etc. Bottom line, I've already researched, and I've seen it all. And what worked for your cousin's neighbor isn't necessarily *our* answer.)
10. "Why don't you have kids yet?" (Good question. Wish I had a good answer.)

Bearing Fruit

I'm sure you can add to the list. Be ready to give an appropriate response to these. They'll come at you all the time. Resist the urge to be sarcastic. (Trust me, I am the queen of sarcasm, but you know it's really, really not nice to answer ignorance that way…at least not in public.)

Day Thirty-Eight

God's Mercy

*"The Pharisee stood up and prayed about himself:
'God, I thank you that I am not like other men.'
But the tax collector would not even look up
to heaven and said, 'God, have mercy on me, a
sinner.' I tell you this man, rather than the other,
went home justified before God.
For everyone who exalts himself will be humbled,
and he who humbles himself will be exalted."*

—Luke 18:11, 13–14

She had a pinched face with pursed lips and haughty eyes. She didn't know me and I don't even remember her name, but I recall clearly her words.

"I am the mother of twin boys and three daughters. You see, I first asked the Lord for a little boy and He blessed me with two at once. Then I asked Him for girls and again He gave me just what I wanted. I'm just spoiled, I guess."

Well now, aren't you special? Apparently, I must be bad, very bad, since the Lord has not given me a boy or a girl—no, not a one. Surely you are most favored. And surely I am punished. Aren't you glad you're not me?

No, that's not what I said to her. And actually, I felt more *sorry* for her than anything. I wonder how she would've responded if I told her I had no children. I sensed arrogance in her, so I imagine she would've regaled me with some fine "wisdom."

I'd rather receive God's mercy than a multitude of children.

Bearing Fruit

When you are slapped in the face with arrogant and ignorant comments, remember that humility brings you God's mercy. Pray for His mercy.

Day Thirty-Nine

Just Like Me

"'I tell you the truth, anyone who will not receive the kingdom of God like a little child will never enter it.' And [Jesus] took the children in his arms, put his hands on them and blessed them."

–Mark 10:15–16

The sweetness of my niece's words soothed the harshness of my infertility.

"When I was in Mommy's tummy, I looked out at all the people and when I saw you, I said, 'I want to be just like her!'"

It's true. Since my niece was a toddler, she has exhibited some of my character. Now, understand, lookswise she is a clone of my sister. She is athletically inclined (inherited from my brother–in–law) and is a talented dancer (genetically passed on from my sister). But when it comes to the amazing technique of crossing her eyes—well, not to brag, but she got *that* from me!

When we get together, the laughter resounds. My sister has a good sense of humor, but she tends to be more on the reserved side. Her daughter leans to a more goofy side—more my style—often to the dismay of my sister. She had to grow up with me and now, in a way, she has to raise a *mini-me*.

God's goodness in this is not lost on me. I have always dreamed of having a daughter. Having such a close relationship with my niece is the next best thing. I don't even have to do the hard work of raising her.

My sister may even one day appreciate our hilarious comedy routines. Well, that might be stretching it.

Bearing Fruit

Don't deny yourself the company of children. Enjoy family and friends' children. Have your nephew or niece spend the night. You'll get all the fun and none of the grunt work!

Day Forty

He Chose Me

"The man said, 'This is now bone of my bones and flesh of my flesh; she shall be called woman, for she was taken out of man.' For this reason a man will leave his father and mother and be united to his wife, and they will become one flesh.
The man and his wife were both naked, and they felt no shame."

—*Genesis 2:23–25*

He could've chosen a domestic queen, but he chose me. He could've chosen a beauty queen, but he chose me. He could've chosen a serious, reserved woman, but he chose me. He could've chosen a rich woman, but he chose me. He could've chosen a quiet, genteel woman, but he chose me.

He might've chosen a fertile woman who could've made him the father of many children, but he chose me. And when we discovered that I was infertile, he could've chosen to leave, but he chose to stay.

My husband has faced this infertility battle with me. Sure, we've had our difficulties and disagreements—but we have weathered the storm together. We've toughed it out. And he has chosen to stick with me.

This crisis has strengthened our bond of love and proven our commitment to each other. I love my husband now more than ever. I love the man he has become. I miss the father he would have been....

I am so glad I chose him. And that he chose me.

Bearing Fruit

Renew your marriage vows. Fall in love all over again. Enjoy a second, third, fourth honeymoon! This is the man the Lord gave you. Be grateful for this love.

PART THREE

Measured Loss: What Infertility Robs You Of

"[I]nfertility is an experience which involves multiple losses. I have come to see six distinct areas of significant loss: 1) Control over many aspects of life, 2) Individual genetic continuity linking , past and future, 3) The joint conception of a child with one's life partner, 4) The physical satisfactions of pregnancy and birth, 5) The emotional gratifications of pregnancy and birth, 6) The opportunity to parent."

— Patricia Irwin Johnson,
from *Adopting after Infertility*

"All my longings lie open before you, O Lord; my sighing is not hidden from you. My heart pounds, my strength fails me; even the light has gone from my eyes."

—Psalm 38:9–10

The losses one faces with infertility are many: control, privacy, the bonding of pregnancy, the joys of parenting, the sweet love of a child. Grieving these losses takes its toll every day. Infertility is a merciless thief.

Day Forty-One

Precious Life

"[David] answered, 'While the child was still alive, I fasted and wept. I thought, "Who knows? The Lord may be gracious to me and let the child live. But now that he is dead, why should I fast? Can I bring him back again? I will go to him, but he will not return to me."'

—2 Samuel 12:22–23

January 16, 1995. The child in my womb died and, little by little, this precious life poured out of me. *When will God bless my womb with life again? Or, will He? There is no way of knowing. All I can do is dry my tears and get on with life.*

God is perfect, God is just, and God is kind. I trust Him. I will wait. I know God can give me the courage to wait.

But it cuts deeply.

We had been trying to conceive for a year and had just started pursuing investigative procedures with my gynecologist. It seemed so perfect of God to grant us this child at such a time. The doctor's office confirmed on a Thursday that I was pregnant. I can still hear the nurse's words.

"You're going to be a mommy!"

On Saturday I chose nutritious foods at the grocery store. And throughout Sunday we told everyone we met that we were expecting.

Then came Monday, January 16. The bleeding began.

I did not weep forever. I could not change what happened. Someday I will go to that child, but that child did not come to me. And so, I wait for what God has planned for us. In January of 1995, it was not His plan for a child.

Be still my soul.

Bearing Fruit

If you've lost a child to miscarriage, identify that child with a name. Shortly after my miscarriage, I had a dream about a baby girl with thick, dark hair like my husband's. In the dream, her name was Abigail and she was our little girl. Maybe this was a dream of the little girl we lost. Whatever the case, since that dream I've named our little lost lamb Abigail. Conceived at the end of December of 1994; died on January 16, 1995. No matter how early in the pregnancy, acknowledging that you miscarried a little person helps tremendously in getting through the grieving process.

Day Forty-Two

Heavenly Restoration

"Now the dwelling of God is with men, and He will live with them. They will be His people, and God Himself will be with them and be their God. He will wipe every tear from their eyes. There will be no more death or mourning or crying or pain,
for the old order of things has passed away. 'I am making everything new!'"

—Revelation 21: 3–4, 5

In heaven, the blind will see, the deaf will hear, and the lame will walk. Those with mental disabilities will be whole. Cancer will be gone; all disease will have disappeared.

But how will my infertility be healed? How will my disability be restored? How will my barren womb suddenly be fruitful?

There is no marriage in heaven; then surely there will be no bearing of children. So what evidence of my restoration will cause me joy in heaven as I am freed from my infertility?

Perhaps I will be assigned to be a *celestial mother* (and I can't wait to meet my little lost Abigail), nurturing and playing with the children of heaven. Maybe it is as James Vernon McGee suggests:

> God will resurrect the infants as they are and… the mother's arms that have ached for them will have the opportunity to hold their little ones. The father who never [held] that little hand will be given that privilege. Children will grow up with their parents.

This is an intriguing and comforting concept. But I cannot know beyond the Bible. And I cannot know beyond my earthly limitations. And for now, I cannot know beyond my infertility.

Except I can know that God is a loving Lord and that certain joy awaits me in heaven, how ever He intends it to be.

Bearing Fruit

This concept of heavenly restoration boggles my mind. How about you? Dig in and research various commentaries. Present your questions on this to your pastor. And then eagerly await the full answers when you reach heaven.

Day Forty-Three

Will it Get Easier?

"The eternal God is your refuge, and underneath are the everlasting arms."

—Deuteronomy 33:27

I'm waiting for it to get easier.

How can I attend a child's first birthday party without feeling empty? How do I react appropriately at the announcement of a new pregnancy or birth? How do I compassionately listen as mothers legitimately share the burdens of raising children? When will my heart not sag when I see a parent and child? When will I go a whole day without infertility crossing my mind?

So far every day brings a struggle of some sort.

My only hiding place is the Lord's everlasting arms. I can only lean on the everlasting arms because leaning on my own understanding has caused me to fall time after time.

Will there ever come a day when it gets easier? I have no idea.

I do know that God will be there with me if it never does.

Bearing Fruit

I remember going through my calendar and when I made note of my niece's fifth birthday, I broke into tears. I have no idea what set that off or why I cried. You will be faced with a certain level of struggle every day because of your childlessness. There's no way to avoid it and often it will hit hard at unexpected moments. Prepare yourself daily with prayer and, when needed, take a time-out in God's everlasting arms.

Day Forty-Four

Where are the Children?

"When Rachel saw that she was not bearing Jacob any children, she became jealous of her sister. So she said to Jacob, 'Give me children, or I'll die!' Jacob became angry with her and said, 'Am I in the place of God, who has kept you from having children?'"

—Genesis 30:1–2

Where are the children?
Why are there no giggles?
No cries in the night?
There are hands poised to tickle…
Arms to comfort…

Where are the children?
Why are the books not being read over and over again?
No sloppy kisses?
There are laps…
Kind faces…

Where are the children?
Why is it so quiet all the time?
No sounds of playing?
There are rooms to fill…
There is money for toys…

Where are the children?
Why is there no one to call me Mommy?
No one to call you Daddy?
There are hearts, longing to parent…
Dreams of tiny hands and feet…

Where are the children?
Not here.

Bearing Fruit

Are you a songwriter? Write a song about your pain. Are you a poet? Write a poem that symbolizes your tears. Are you an artist? Paint a picture that portrays what you are missing. Are you a photographer? Capture an image that expresses your heartache. Whatever outlet you enjoy, use it to express creatively what your body cannot.

Day Forty-Five

Miscarrying

"'For I know the plans I have for you,' declares the Lord, 'plans to prosper you and not to harm you, plans to give you hope and a future.'"

—Jeremiah 29:11

In the bathroom, I moaned in pain. My tears mingled with sweat.

I was miscarrying after only a few weeks of pregnancy. It sickened me as I realized I was flushing this little life down the toilet.

What cruelty! What heartache!

In the midst of my pain, I wondered where my kind and loving Father God was.

As I doubled over with cramps I looked up to see a verse printed on a potpourri bag that was given to me by a friend. It was Jeremiah 29:11. "For I know the plans I have for you. Plans to prosper you and not to harm you, plans to give you a hope and a future."

This was God's comforting reply to me. His plans were not to harm me but to give me hope and a future. He was painfully aware of my grief. He was painfully aware of the loss of life.

He kissed me with the words from Jeremiah and I was comforted.

Bearing Fruit

There are no adequate words to comfort someone who has lost a child. This has to be one of the most devastating heartaches to endure. Only the love of God can comfort at such a time. If you know someone facing this pain, speak no words; just be there. If you face this pain, know that God is there.

Day Forty-Six

Losing a Little Lamb

"He tends His flock like a shepherd: He gathers the lambs in His arms and carries them close to His heart."

—Isaiah 40:11

Consider this thought-provoking concept shared by Reverend James Vernon McGee:

> When a shepherd seeks to lead his sheep to better grass up the winding, thorny mountain paths, he often finds that the sheep will not follow him. They fear the unknown ridges and the sharp rocks. The shepherd will then reach into the flock and take a little lamb. Soon the…mother sheep begins to follow, and afterward comes the entire flock. They ascend the torturous path to greener pastures. So it is with the Good Shepherd. Sometimes He reaches into the flock and takes a little lamb to Himself. He uses the experience to lead His people, to lift them to new heights of commitment as they follow the little lamb all the way home.

I miscarried the only little lamb God has given me so far. My heart received some comfort from this scenario. Jesus is the Good Shepherd, caring deeply for all His flock. He holds my little lamb in His arms. I trust Him as I follow Him up the precarious path.

He leads me to a higher level of trust and faith. At the end of the journey I will be rewarded with a joyous reunion with my little lamb.

Bearing Fruit

If you've lost a little lamb, pray that the Good Shepherd will lead you to new heights of trust and commitment.

Day Forty-Seven

"Buttercup"

"How long, O Lord? Will you forget me forever? How long will you hide your face from me? How long must I wrestle with my thoughts and every day have sorrow in my heart?
But I trust in your unfailing love; my heart rejoices in your salvation.
I will sing to the Lord, for he has been good to me."

—Psalm 13:1–2, 5–6

I was distracted by the cries of a child in the hallway that pierced the work environment, as well as my heart. It made me think of how rarely I hear a child crying. A seasoned mother might scoff at that statement, gladly offering to take my place for a while.

The incessant crying drew me to the hallway. There she was, an inconsolable little toddler in the arms of a nursery worker. On a whim I started singing the 1960s pop hit, "Buttercup." This song has a catchy tune, as the lovestruck fellow asks Buttercup why she builds him up just to let him down. He then insists he continues to love her despite how she treats him and begs her not to break his heart.

The crying child was entranced with my singing (too young to know quality) and enamored with my dancing (or did I remind her of Big Bird?) She wanted to come to me. She cuddled in my arms. I sang "Buttercup" softly in her ear.

She had no idea the symbolism behind the words.

She had no concept that I sang, not just out of an entertaining spirit, but out of a pseudo-prophetic statement of my disappointment that I might never entertain a child of my own.

Deep down, I sang to God, asking why He would build up my hopes of being a mommy just to let me down.

"I need *you* more than anyone, baby. You know that I have from the start. So build me up, Buttercup, but don't break my heart...."

Bearing Fruit

The Lord's voice comes in the most unlikely ways sometimes. Look for the humor in the dark times. Belt out a few of your favorite songs to lift your heart. And never pass up the chance to cuddle a child.

Day Forty-Eight

Suffering

"And the God of all grace, who called you to His eternal glory in Christ, after you have suffered a little while, will Himself restore you and make you strong, firm, and steadfast."

—I Peter 5:10

Suffering the disgrace of infertility is so difficult.

Feels as though I am the mother of a child named *infertility*. This child given to me is a troubled child—unruly, disrespectful, never giving a mother peace. It plagues me, haunts me, envelops me, and surrounds me. I feel trapped by suffering. Hyperventilating. *When will it end? When will my heart be lifted?* God has not given me the child I've prayed for, cried for, and so desired. Instead He gives me suffering. I am beaten down, broken up. I feel as though I'll never be myself again.

How do I discipline this unruly "child?"

As it is with parenthood, I stand firm on what I know is true. Parents attempt to instill truths into their children, and sometimes that means experiencing a broken heart. There are tears and heartache in both motherhood and childlessness.

But, God has promised that I will suffer only "a little while." After that, God Himself will see to it that I am strong again in Him. *I will stand firm again in Him. I will stay steadfast in Him.*

I will be restored.

Bearing Fruit

Suffering is a high calling from God. You may not like to hear that, but it's true. See it for what it truly is. God promises restoration. Stand firm and pray for that. You *will* be restored.

Day Forty-Nine

Tree-Topper

"While they were there, the time came for the baby to be born, and she gave birth to her firstborn, a son. She wrapped him in cloths and placed him in a manger, because there was no room for them in the inn."

—Luke 2:6–7

My husband and I were married in May of 1992. That first Christmas we put up our tree and suddenly realized we had no tree-topper. I spoke excitedly.

"Let's get our first tree-topper when we have our first child!" My husband found that to be a little odd, but agreed to the idea.

The following Christmas we were beginning infertility tests since we had been trying to get pregnant for a year. We still had not purchased the tree-topper.

Amazingly, some time during that Christmas week we finally conceived. Sadly, this conception ended in a miscarriage and our little dream went to heaven.

By our third Christmas together we were still childless. The Lord spoke to me in the middle of a bustling mall.

"The most important baby that will ever be born has been born."

My heart was lifted and I purchased a star to top our tree in honor of a baby born in a stable, born to die for me.

Bearing Fruit

Christmas can be difficult because it is so commercially geared to children... the happy, large family gathered round the tree. Remember whose birth we celebrate—the Savior of the World! Now, that's a birth even an infertile couple can celebrate.

Day Fifty

I Love Children

"Jesus said, 'Let the little children come to me,
and do not hinder them,
for the kingdom of heaven belongs to such as these.'
When he had placed his hands on them, he went on from there."

—Matthew 19:14–15

I pause to look at a baby's smile.
There, I see it's all worthwhile.
I see an innocence that only God can give.

In that sweet, little face I see,
All the love God has for me.
And I can't bring myself to look away.

Sweet baby smile,
Frozen in a frame,
I have labored long and hard beneath my pain.
But in her dancing eyes I know,
Eternity's forever-glow,
And just like a parent's arms, my Father God won't let me go.

Let the little children come to me! I love children. I have enjoyed the company of children since I was a young teen. Why should I allow my infertility to rob me of those sweet little people? I look for the "spiritual children" God has placed in my life and take pleasure in that, instead of allowing the gift of them to magnify what I do not have.

The Lord Jesus was childless.

Now I understand the many theological and practical reasons for this, but it still gives me a sense of comfort. I know He can relate to my pain as no child on earth ever called Him "Daddy." Yet He surrounded Himself with children. He loved them and spoke highly of them. I, in my childlessness, need to follow His lead and do the same.

Let the little children come to me!

Bearing Fruit

Whoa! Jesus was childless. Can you let that thought comfort you? Do not let infertility hinder children from blessing your life. And think of the joy it brings to the Lord Jesus' heart when we call Him Abba (Daddy) Father. In His thirty-three years on earth, He never heard a child call Him that. But, go on, call on "Abba Daddy" now.

Day Fifty-One

Lady-in-Waiting

"Give ear to my words, O Lord, consider my sighing. Listen to my cry for help, my King and my God, for to you I pray. In the morning, O Lord, you hear my voice; in the morning I lay my requests before you and wait in expectation."

—Psalm 5:1–3

A giant billboard asks, "Expecting a Baby?"

Why, yes, as a matter of fact, I've been expecting a baby for about ten years now. Month- after-month, year-after-year spent in expectation of a baby to add to our family.

I'm still waiting. Still expecting God to pull off another Abraham/Sarah maneuver.

But, so far, no one to name. To feed. To cuddle. To nurture. To discipline. To love. To laugh at. To cry over.

No one to name.

Will I ever stop waiting? Will I ever stop hoping? Will I ever stop dreaming?

I guess it's OK to dream if dreams don't interfere with the present. I guess it's OK to hope if hopes don't give into despair. And I have no choice in waiting, but I must not allow the waiting to disrupt my living.

There may yet come a day when a little child enters our lives, and we can say, "Welcome. We've been expecting you!"

Bearing Fruit

If you are detailed-oriented, you may want to get Wishing for a Baby: A Preconception Journal, *published by Conceiving Concepts, Inc. It is a pragmatic way to catalogue each step of the way in your baby-quest.*

Day Fifty-Two

Damaged for Good

"[What was] intended to harm me...God intended it for good, to accomplish what is now being done."

—Genesis 50:20

Damaged goods. That's how I feel at times with this waiting womb. This useless uterus, these futile fallopian tubes, these oddball ovaries. They do not function as God designed. They are *damaged goods.*

In *The Empty Cradle: Infertility in America from Colonial Times to the Present,* by Margaret Marsh and Wanda Ronner, the authors note how doctors once believed "a woman's reproductive system was like a machine, either functioning well or in need of repair." Sometimes I felt like a car, and my doctor is a mechanic looking under the hood to see which parts are in working order and which parts needed a tune-up.

That is my negative perspective, however. God's perspective is far more positive, more spiritually optimistic. He intends that my infertility be used for good. He already has shown His purposes behind my infertility in reaching out to those who suffer. Each time He uses me in some magnificent, miraculous way, it becomes clearer. I am not damaged goods but "damaged for good!" Ultimately, He intends to use this pain for good.

Damaged for *good.*

Bearing Fruit

You *are* damaged for good—for God's good. *I'm not saying He caused it, but He will bend it to accomplish good. Ask Him to show you how He can use your infertility for a good purpose.*

Day Fifty-Three

You Go to Breakfast!

"You turned my wailing into dancing; you removed my sackcloth and clothed me with joy, that my heart may sing to you and not be silent. O Lord my God, I will give thanks to you forever."

—Psalm 30:11–12

You go to breakfast!

I encouraged a fellow infertile to do this after she had been bummed out from baby dedications at church and didn't want to follow through on plans to go out with friends.

Man, I get so sick of infertility robbing my joy. I get so tired of missing out on the little life-celebrations just because I'm barren. One of the most gloriously miraculous things in life is a child and because I am denied my own I often deny myself the enjoyment of other children.

Well, I'm tired of being bound to that sadness.

I want to have fun!

I want to breathe in that sweet baby scent.

I want to get a big ol' squeezing hug and a sloppy, slobbery kiss from a toddler.

I want to make kids giggle until they hiccup.

I want to enjoy the children I do have in my life, even though they are not my own.

And after baby dedications at church, infertile couples should go out to breakfast and enjoy their lives!

You go to breakfast!

Bearing Fruit

Infertility is a thief, a merciless joy-robber. There may be times you almost need to force yourself to be with children. But do it! A child's lighthearted and innocent ways will chase away the infertility stalker. If something bums you out and brings you down, shake it off and follow through on fun plans. You go, girl!

Day Fifty-Four

Handprints on My Heart

"At that time the disciples came to Jesus and asked, 'Who is the greatest in the kingdom of heaven?' He called a little child and had him stand among them. And he said, 'I tell you the truth, unless you change and become like little children, you will never enter the kingdom of heaven. Therefore, whoever humbles himself like this child is the greatest in the kingdom of heaven. And whoever welcomes a little child like this in my name welcomes me.'"

—Matthew 18:1–5

Each time a child hugs me,
He leaves tiny handprints on my heart.
I never wipe them clean.
I leave them there to cover the pain of my childlessness.

Each time a child kisses me,
She leaves tiny lip prints on my soul.
I never wipe them off,
I leave them there to cover the anger at my childlessness.

Each time children infiltrate my world,
They leave tiny footprints in my mind.

I never wipe them out.

I leave them there to cover the emptiness of my childlessness.

I take all the child-time I can get! I love those little people. They bring joy to my world. Even in the darkest throes of my infertility I knew I would never stop loving kids. Their innocence covers the injustice of infertility.

Bearing Fruit

Do I sound like a broken record? Fill your world with children! Now, you may need to go through a time of grieving as you adjust to your infertility, and there will be times when the realization of what you are missing will hit hard. But the Lord Jesus said to welcome these little ones in His Name, and you will find that their uninhibited love will melt your heart again and again.

Day Fifty-Five

Mother Appointed by God

"Sing, O barren woman, you who never bore a child; burst into song, shout for joy, you who were never in labor; because more are the children of the desolate woman than of her who has a husband."

—Isaiah 54:1

What song would a barren woman sing? How could she shout for joy? I think I know....

Mine is a worthless womb,
Never a child to bear,
God had a different plan,
Leaving my heart to tear.

Giving more of Himself,
Taking all of my pain,
Letting obsession go,
Throwing off all my strain.

Wiping away my tears,
Casting vision to see,
God showed many a child,
Holding and loving me.

This then I shout for joy,
Truly it may sound odd:
"Blessed is this barren womb,
Mother proclaimed by God!"

God appoints most natural mothers, but sadly some mothers are simply a biological incident. Good mothers are surely blessed and are pleasing to God. Others don't deserve to claim the name of *Mother.*

On the flip side, many amazing women are denied natural births. But God goes beyond this by appointing them as adoptive mothers and most definitely as spiritual mothers.

So, barren woman, let go of the pain of no labor pains and open your eyes to the children around you that God has appointed you to impact their young lives.

Bearing Fruit

God has put children in your life. Even if you never have your own, or never choose to adopt, you still are appointed to exemplify godliness before little eyes watching you from afar. Maybe God is calling you to teach a Sunday School class. You can witness spiritual rebirths if not natural ones.

Day Fifty-Six

The Benefit of this Anguish

"I cried like a swift or thrush, I moaned like a mourning dove.
My eyes grew weak as I looked to the heavens. I am troubled; O Lord, come to my aid!
But what can I say? He has spoken to me, and he himself has done this.
I will walk humbly all my years because of this anguish of my soul.
Lord, by such things men live; and my spirit finds life in them too. You restored me to health and let me live. Surely it was for my benefit that I suffered such anguish."

—Isaiah 38:14–17

The Lord allowed this. He allowed my husband and me to marry. He allowed us to dream of becoming parents. He has allowed my body to remain infertile.

I have cried. I have moaned. Others live with this same anguish. Some do it better than me; some worse.

Surely, this is for my benefit, Lord. When day after day I feel the dull ache—will I ever not think of it? Will I ever go through a day free of the pain? Surely there is purpose in this! Surely I will see the blessing. Surely I will find the grace to thank You for my empty arms.

Surely I will not bemoan forever that no one calls me "Mommy." Surely I will clearly see the benefit of this anguish....

Right, Lord? Lord? Lord?

Bearing Fruit

The Lord has allowed your infertility. It is humbling. There is anguish. Bottom line: Often in your anguish you find the very best of God as you humbly seek Him.

Day Fifty-Seven

The Great Responsibility of Parenthood

"My son, keep your father's commands and do not forsake your mother's teaching.
Bind them upon your heart forever; fasten them around your neck.
When you walk, they will guide you; when you sleep, they will watch over you;
when you awake, they will speak to you."

—*Proverbs 6:20–22*

To see a little one, a young life—whether infant, toddler, young child, teen—the thought will cross my mind: *It doesn't seem possible that I can go through life not watching a little person grow up, take shape, define character, become a man or woman, and know that I had a direct impact on the outcome.*

A parent is the lifeblood that flows through the veins of a child, pumping the heart of who that child is and who that child will become. This is God's great responsibility and magnificent charge to those who bear the title "mother" or "father." Granted, some fail in this task, but many do their best. None do it without some measure of regret. All will answer to God as to how they fulfilled their role.

Often I look with sadness upon a child, wishing I could undertake this magnificent charge, to bear the task of growing a productive human being.

Of course, along with this magnificent charge come the not-so-glamorous points of parenthood. A friend described this touching scene: "Mounds of laundry, mud tracked on a clean floor, countless nights of cleaning up after upset stomachs that are unexpectedly emptied, doctor bills, or paying for orthodontia, or sitting in the freezing rain at high school football games...."

She could've gone on, but I jumped in my sports car and went shopping, free as a bird.

Bearing Fruit

It's true. You don't have the blessing of parenthood, but neither do you have the burden. Pray for parents that you know. Help them out when you can by offering to take their kids for an evening.

Day Fifty-Eight

This Womb is Mine...Barren

"On the first day of the week, very early in the morning, the women took the spices they had prepared and went to the tomb. They found the stone rolled away from the tomb, but when they entered, they did not find the body of the Lord Jesus. While they were wondering about this, suddenly two men in clothes that gleamed like lightning stood beside them. In their fright the women bowed down with their faces to the ground, but the men said to them, 'Why do you look for the living among the dead? He is not here; he has risen."

—Luke 24:1–7

This womb is cavernous.

This womb is lonely.

No child will form there, grow there, be nourished there.

This womb is silent.

No heartbeat, no movement.

This womb is unused, woeful.

This womb is mine, barren.

His tomb is cavernous.

His tomb is empty.

No body will decay there, rot there, decompose there.

His tomb is silent.

Except for angels, an announcement, a question:

"Why do you look for the living among the dead?"

I pondered this as I pondered the deadness of my womb...

Leave the womb, and weep no more.

Rise and seek the Living Lord!

Do not mourn this barren womb.

Celebrate the Empty Tomb!

Bearing Fruit

Resurrection life has far greater value than earthly life. Do you have Christ's gift of eternal life? If you do, celebrate with me. If you are not sure, don't wait any longer. Read the book of John. Read Romans 5:8–11. Don't waste another minute without Christ in it.

Day Fifty-Nine

Half a Uterus?

"As you do not know the path of the wind, or how the body is formed in a mother's womb, so you cannot understand the work of God, the Maker of all things."

—Ecclesiastes 11:5

Did anyone ever tell you that you have half a uterus?"

A hysterosalpingogram (HSG) had somehow turned into a nightmare.

The HSG is a standard procedure for checking fallopian tubes and other related reproductive parts. But this was turning out differently from the HSG I had had a few years earlier. This one was horribly painful. In the past there was some mild cramping, but nothing like what I was experiencing now. As a result they hurried, trying to get through the procedure.

A doctor kept asking me questions about past surgeries. Then as I lay there exhausted from the pain, he piped up with the question.

"Did anyone ever tell you that you have half a uterus?"

Really now! I think I would've remembered if someone had told me I had half a uterus. He offered no sympathetic words. He left the room but his haunting question lingered. I held in the tears until my husband and I made it to the car. We looked at each other with shock and dismay.

We had to wait two weeks for the appointment where our doctor could go over the HSG results. Two weeks of despondency, disbelief, and struggle. Two weeks of endless questions....

Why would God make me this way? Will we ever be able to conceive a child? Why hadn't someone diagnosed this sooner? Why had this happened? Why? Why? Why?

At the appointment our doctor began to discuss the test results. Then he suddenly paused as he studied the X-rays more closely. He conferred with the intern in the office, who was at the HSG. In hushed tones she verified that I had been in much pain during the procedure.

The doctor then shifted into doubletalk. But my husband and I gathered this: Because of the difficulty I was having, they were able to get the scope in only so far. So they could only see half the picture—thus the illusion of half a uterus. We were relieved. But I was still miffed at the unprofessional manner of the doctor on the day of the procedure.

Despite the amazing advances of the medical field, humans are bound to err. No matter what we hope to accomplish medically, the Lord Creator is the Master Designer. We can prod and probe all we want into scientific wonders, but they remain just that: wonders.

Conception and pregnancy remain miracles and though we look to our doctors for answers, we must ultimately look to the Master Designer for truth.

Bearing Fruit

Your doctor is not God. Don't allow any medical expert to push you to do something if you are uncomfortable taking that step. Also, remember God is the Creator and Designer of your body.

Day Sixty

It's Midnight

"I am worn out from groaning; all night long I flood my bed with weeping and drench my couch with tears. My eyes grow weak with sorrow; they fail because of all my foes. Away from me, all you who do evil, for the Lord has heard my weeping.
The Lord has heard my cry for mercy; the Lord accepts my prayer."

—Psalm 6:6–9

It's midnight. Do you know where your children are?"

This is an oft-repeated line from a public service announcement that ran on television some years ago.

There have been some restless nights as I've wondered where *my* children are. Why hasn't God given me any children? I've wrestled with God in anger over the disillusionment of this injustice.

My Heavenly Father has never turned His back to my cries. Instead, He's listened patiently to my complaints. He's comforted me and not judged me. At times I listen to the lies of Satan and sink deeper. But God stays in the midst of my pain and offers the truth of His love. My enemies flee.

He hears and He knows.

It's midnight and He knows where His child is. And He is there with her.

Bearing Fruit

Maybe this is a sleepless night for you. When you have such nights, don't stay in bed and toss in the darkness. The voices of fear and frustration will only get louder. Get up, turn a little light on, and snuggle under an afghan on the couch with your Bible. Weep softly if you need to, and plead for God to comfort you. Ask Him to grant that His Word might whisper a sweet lullaby so you can head back to the silent sleep of your bed.

PART FOUR

Multiplied Grace: How God Blesses and Strengthens

"No one can fully comprehend why God acts in particular ways or what He intends to accomplish. We can be sure, though, that infertility does not mean we are being punished. On the contrary, the Bible assures us of God's love for us.
He does not always change the difficult circumstances of our lives, but he offers us strength and courage to meet them."

— Beth Spring, from Childless

"Let us then approach the throne of grace with confidence,
so that we may receive mercy
and find grace to help us in our time of need."

—Hebrews 4:16

Let's focus on finding that God's grace is sufficient. A childless woman can seek other pursuits, other dreams, and try to put the pain of infertility behind her. Yet only God can fill the void. Only God is the salve to mend the brokenness that barrenness brings.

Day Sixty-One

My Family Tree is a Barren Tree

"I am the true vine, and my Father is the gardener. He cuts off every branch in me that bears no fruit, while every branch that does bear fruit he prunes so that it will be even more fruitful.
You are already clean because of the word I have spoken to you. Remain in me, and I will remain in you. No branch can bear fruit by itself; it must remain in the vine. Neither can you bear fruit unless you remain in me. This is to my Father's glory, that you bear much fruit, showing yourselves to be my disciples. You did not choose me, but I chose you and appointed you to go and bear fruit—fruit that will last."

—John 15:1–4, 8, 16

My family tree is a barren tree.

There are no branches springing forth from me.
Progeny, heredity. These are foreign words to me.

My gene pool is dried up.
My bloodline cut off.

No namesake to name;
No heritage to claim.

My quiver is pathetically empty.
My family tree is a barren tree.

My spiritual tree is a fruitful tree.

Fruit hangs from its branches bountifully.
Godliness, faithfulness: these are familiar words to me.
My fount of love flows.
His Bloodline of forgiveness flows through me.

I bear Christ's Name;
His heritage I claim.

My cup pours forth abundantly.
My spiritual tree is a fruitful tree.

Bearing Fruit

As a believer, you are to bear spiritual fruit. You can bear spiritual fruit in some way every day. Remain in Christ Jesus and be fruitful!

Day Sixty-Two

Pain and Praise

"For the word of the Lord is right and true; He is faithful in all He does.
We wait in hope for the Lord; He is our help and our shield.
In Him our hearts rejoice, for we trust in His holy name."

—Psalm 33:4, 20–21

How do I rejoice in my infertility? I wonder.

I can praise God despite the disappointment. I can trust Him with my whole heart. He is my help and my shield. He sustains me with His Word. I believe what He says is true. He is faithful and fills me with faith to overflowing.

Building anything takes time and effort. When building a new home, people generally put forth great time and effort. The materials must be strong in order to stand against the elements of nature. And when the construction is complete, the builder can rejoice at the finished work.

The pain of any circumstance builds faith. Joy, the kind given only by the Holy Spirit, is needed to stand against the torrents of any trial. That doesn't make the pain easier, but it does give it some value—some meaning, and some purpose. Praise gives us the stamina to go on despite obstacles. With trust and hope, we decorate our countenance.

Only the strong help and shield of the Lord fortifies my faith. Only praise can beautify pain.

Bearing Fruit

Sing praise songs to God. Belt them out! If you're like me, it's better to do that when you're alone in the car. Let your heart sing out to God. Praise songs ease the pain.

Day Sixty-Three

Alright!

"Carry each other's burdens, and in this way you will fulfill the law of Christ."

—*Galatians 6:2*

I experienced a particularly difficult time in my journey of infertility. An *oppressed* feeling existed in my heart—a feeling I could not shake! After a few weeks of struggle the depression finally came to a head in an amazing time of prayer and tears with my friend.

We grasped hands and prayed fervently. We choked out words of praise, thanksgiving, repentance, and intercession. We cried tears of compassion and of deep spiritual understanding.

Funny how a good cry can cure a bad depression.

It was amazing to share each other's pain. I had never before experienced such a quick lifting of my heart. The Lord reached down and lifted a great burden from my shoulders.

I ended our prayer with, "Alright." Then we laughed.

It seemed odd. Maybe God was saying that it would be alright. He *makes* it all right. He makes *us* "all right." And, one day, *all* will be *right*.

Alright!

Bearing Fruit

Everyone has some measure of pain. Everyone is suffering a trial of some sort. Get together with someone whom you trust. Be vulnerable with each other. Go before the Lord with each other's burdens.

Day Sixty-Four

Seek to Mend

"Blessed is the man who perseveres under trial,
because when he has stood the test,
he will receive the crown of life that God has
promised to those who love him,"

—James 1:12

I have coats, pants, and shirts that are missing buttons or that have a slight tear in the seam or some such basic mending need. *Why do they continue to pile up in the spare room?* I just don't take the time to mend them. I live in a "throwaway" society, a fast paced, no-time-to-fix-it culture. I simply replace what's broken.

I don't mend; I end.

It seems this habit filters into other areas of life, too. Through some of the harder times of my infertility, I have often wanted to just give up. Give up on my marriage; give up on trying to conceive; yes, even give up on life.

It's clear in the Bible that the Lord requires diligence and perseverance. I must persevere, no matter what obstacles seem to intrude. I cannot give up at every bump in the road. And when I persevere just enough to get through to the next day, I find that the road is a little less rocky. I find the Lord's light shining a little brighter and my load is lightened.

Sewing on a few buttons reminds me to mend, not end, in other areas of my life, also.

Bearing Fruit

Do you have some mending to do? Take care of it! You'll feel a sense of completion. Let it remind you to persevere.

Day Sixty-Five

Every Sunday

"Praise be to the God and Father of our Lord Jesus Christ,
the Father of compassion and the God of all comfort."

—2 Corinthians 1:3

Every Sunday at church I walk by the nursery suite. But that is all I do—walk by. No child waits there for me, to reach for me, to put a little hand in my safe *Mommy-hand* as we go down the hall. No, I just walk by.

Infertility is a diagnosis my husband and I face month after month. Expectations rise and then crash; we are left to deal with the disappointment. Others find it difficult to relate to our pain. How can we cringe at the blessed news of a coming birth? It is easy to see why we have few sympathizers.

Where can I turn but to my heavenly Father? He understands the heaviness of my heart. He knows the intensity of my sorrow. He strengthens my weary soul. It is a heavy burden at times to walk by the nursery and hear the giggles, the crying, and the cooing. My heart sinks at the sight of mothers happily carrying their babies. But, you know, I never take an alternate route.

Yes, I walk by the nursery suite every Sunday.

And the *God of all Comfort* walks beside me.

Bearing Fruit

It's often lonely to be infertile. It's difficult for others to understand the depth of our pain unless they have experienced it on some level themselves. Even then, our own pain and infertility story is unique to each of us. It is of great comfort to know that the "God of all Comfort" walks with us.

Day Sixty-Six

Little Angel

"And whoever welcomes a little child like this in my name welcomes me.
See that you do not look down on one of these little ones.
For I tell you that their angels in heaven always see the face of my Father in heaven."

—Matthew 18:5, 10

Every now and then, God gives me a little surprise gift.

A host of little kids crowded outside my office in search of M&Ms®. I have a silly little dispenser that provides a fun way to get candy. So I took my dispenser out in the hallway and three little toddler boys received the candy.

Then a sweet-faced angel of a girl toddled over. She stood back, awestruck at the momentous candy event. As I sat on a chair she came over and nonchalantly leaned against my legs, fascinated by the candy dispenser. I handed her a few M&Ms, and she received them. Then, in one of those moments that take your breath away, she leaned her soft cheek against my hand.

The affection of little ones is rare these days.

How perfect of God to do that for me.

Bearing Fruit

Welcome little children into your world. Treasure those little moments. Store them in your heart for later reference. Thank God for them.

Day Sixty-Seven

God's Song

"The Lord your God is with you, he is mighty to save. He will take great delight in you, he will quiet you with his love, he will rejoice over you with singing."

—Zephaniah 3:17

Did it have to be the week before Mother's Day that I would have false hopes of being pregnant? I mean, c'mon. That seemed like rotten planning....

I hadn't been "late" for quite awhile. *So, why? Why go through getting the pregnancy test, only to see "one line"*—the typical, "Sorry—this is not a winner; try again" result. You'd think the Lord would have cut me some slack.

Is Mother's Day not already painful enough? I protested. It seemed cruel for the Lord to let my hopes build right before Mother's Day— like a practical joke or something. I felt scoffed at, like a kid being teased on the playground. God seemed like a bully. I couldn't make sense of it. I didn't see His Hand in it at all. I was heartbroken.

Then came Mother's Day.

In church we sang one of my favorite worship songs. The lyrics were quite simple.

He will rejoice over you.

If you could only hear His Voice, you would hear the Lord rejoice.

Rejoicing over you with singing….

Twice in the past I had sung that song as a prayer for specific people in my life who were going through severe trials. As I sang it that Mother's Day, I wondered, *Should I pray this for someone?*

God answered.

"Let Me sing it to *you*," He seemed to say.

My anger and confusion dissipated instantly as the Lord quieted my heart with His love.

It was the best Mother's Day ever.

Bearing Fruit

Let praise songs lift you. Let God sing them to you. Sing them to Him! Blast them on the car stereo or at home when you're feeling down. Song will quiet your anguished soul.

Day Sixty-Eight

Trace God's Grace

"[Jesus] is the image of the invisible God...we proclaim Him, admonishing and teaching everyone with all wisdom so that we may present everyone perfect in Christ."

—Colossians 1:15, 28

Remember tracing books? A line drawing of some sort—maybe a cartoon character, or a dog, or a house—lay under the trace paper placed over top of the image. You'd trace the image onto the tracing paper. Though you were not the originator, you could create a good replica of the image as you "drew" and, also, if you did it consistently it would improve your drawing skill since the practice would teach you to control line movements.

I want to trace God's grace.

I can put tracing paper over His Word and replicate the grace that is shown there. I look to believers of times past who have left a record of their understanding of God's grace. Or I look at a few believers in my life right now that exhibit grace.

Tracing grace gives me a replica, a model to shoot for. I can never conjure up grace from within myself. God is the Originator of it. And, over time,

I will improve my response time to receiving grace or to giving grace.

I want to trace God's grace.

Bearing Fruit

Study Abraham in Genesis 12–25, Joseph in Genesis 37–50, or Paul in 2 Corinthians 11–12. How did God's grace show in their circumstances? Do you know someone who has faced trials, letting God's grace show through their pain? Meet with that person and "trace" the grace they exhibit.

Day Sixty-Nine

Power in Weakness

"But [the Lord] said to me, "My grace is sufficient for you, for my power is made perfect in weakness." Therefore, I will boast all the more gladly about my weaknesses, so that Christ's power may rest on me."

—2 Corinthians 12:9

I'm not sure that God said, "Vicki Caswell will be infertile for a purpose."

Life presents many opportunities to experience pain. That's the law of the land. That's the consequence of living in a fallen world. So I'm not convinced God caused my infertility. But I do know I can find purpose in the pain.

I should not focus on the difficulty itself—my infertility. I have racked my brain over and over, trying to figure out why God would prohibit us from having children. I haven't found an answer. It never makes sense to me. But the pain leads me to His sufficient grace. That is His purpose!

Yes, I can delight in the weakness of my infertility, not because of its existence but because the pain has given me opportunity to comfort others, to show Christ's power in my weaknesses.

Bearing Fruit

Any pain can have purpose. Seek out someone who is suffering some trial and offer encouragement. Encourage by telling others how God gets you through your trials.

Day Seventy

Gushing Grace

"And God is able to make all grace abound to you, so that in all things at all times, having all that you need...."

—2 Corinthians 9:8

It was starting to sink in. Putting the dishes in the dishwasher, I had a thought that crashed in on me: *It's never gonna happen. That child I've dreamed of most of my life does not exist, will not exist.*

I felt my heart drop with a thud.

Will I, can I find contentment? Am I doomed to experience unexpected moments of sadness for the rest of my life? Sure, I can go on to chase other goals, achieve success in other ways, but will it ever be enough? No, it can't cover that spot named "infertility." Only one thing can....

If I do not find sufficiency in God, I will never be satisfied. There will always be an ache, a longing, a void. Nothing on this earth will soothe. No one on this earth can love completely. I am far too demanding; my expectations too numerous. Only an infinite God can love me to overflowing.

One thing is enough: His grace.

I long to grab gobs and gobs of His grace and immerse myself in its gushing warmth. I long for it to wash over me like a refreshing shower.

That's how I want to experience God's grace. He gives living water—free, fast-flowing, fresh, forever!

Wash over me, grace, gushing grace.

Bearing Fruit

Do a word study on the concept of grace in the Bible. Ask God for more of His grace. Give some of it away.

Day Seventy-One

Our Furry Child

"A righteous man cares for the needs of his animal."

—Proverbs 12:10

No, I don't dress my dog in baby clothes and take her out in a baby buggy, but she has been a special blessing to my husband and me. We do, however, call Sadie our "furry child," and if a child ever does come along, our dog will surely be wondering how she lost her princess status.

Frankly, pets of infertile couples have it made. We tend to express all the love we want to give to a child toward our ever-loyal, small animals. We get them gifts for their birthday and Christmas. Some folks even take their pet to have a picture taken with Santa!

Sadie's love has soothed my heartache many times as I have pined for a baby. Her sweet eyes have looked at me and touched a tender spot.

I'm thankful God has used an eighty-five pound dog to minister to me in my pain. And Sadie never expects much more in return than a belly scratch.

Bearing Fruit

If you don't already have one, consider getting a pet or two. They can ease your pain and give you an outlet for all that love you are saving for a child. If you have a pet, thank God for this gift and give your "furry child" a good belly scratch.

Day Seventy-Two

Soaring Above the Drudge

"I said, 'Oh, that I had wings of a dove! I would fly away and be at rest—
I would flee far away.' But I call to God and the Lord saves me.
Cast your cares on the Lord and He will sustain you."

–Psalm 55:6–7, 16, 22

I do not want to *dredge through the drudge*, as is my custom, but rather to bathe myself in the light of the Lord's Presence so that I rise above the drudge and never even consider its presence.

Why do I not grasp the gift of life God has given? Why do I begrudge this spot in eternity and sludge through it as though it were some great burden?

Lord, show me the magnificence of the moment, my moment in eternity!

I need to be founded and grounded in Him. I want to rise above the aches and complaints of the physical and rise to the spiritual, the clean, the sanctified!

Hannah Whitall Smith challenges the believer to fly on the "wings of surrender and trust." She tells how one woman learned to fly on such wings after an endless trial she could not escape. She tells readers that, "during the long years of trial, her wings grew so strong from constant flying that...when the trials were at their hardest...her soul was carried over them on a beautiful rainbow and found itself in a peaceful resting place on the other side."

The Holy Spirit soars above the muck and mire.

Lift me there, Lord!

I find I cannot fly without Him.

Bearing Fruit

Read Hannah Whitall Smith's classic book, The Christian's Secret of a Happy Life, *and see how one woman got "up above the clouds."*

Day Seventy-Three

Don't Let Go

"So Jacob was left alone, and a man wrestled with him till daybreak. When the man saw that he could not overpower him, he touched the socket of Jacob's hip so that his hip was wrenched as he wrestled with the man. Then the man said, 'Let me go, for it is daybreak.'
But Jacob replied, 'I will not let you go unless you bless me.'"

—*Genesis 32:24–26*

W*as Jacob wrong to wrestle with God?* I don't believe so.

Jacob was a deceiver and manipulated circumstances in order to get what he wanted. This wrestling match changed all that. He learned he must depend on the Lord and not on his own cleverness. He learned the value of holding on to the Lord through difficult circumstances.

"I will not let go unless You bless me," Jacob said.

How often have I cried the same thing to God? I must hold on to the Lord with everything I've got. He shows me that He is the One with Whom I must wrestle. The tough times filter through His Hand, and it is His Hand I must reach for and not let go until I am blessed.

Does this mean that because of my insistence I must be blessed by God with a child?

No. Now that would be a wonderful blessing, but it is not the only blessing I can receive from His Hand. The ultimate blessing is the Lord Himself and His magnificent love.

I will not let go of that!

Bearing Fruit

The Lord is the only stability. Hold on to Him and don't let go. *God may wrench your heart in the process. Pray with your spouse and together ask the Lord to bless you. Accept that your blessing may not come in the form of a child, but that an answer and a blessing* will *come. God promised.*

Day Seventy-Four

Pick Up the Phone!

"We have different gifts, according to the grace given us.
If it is encouraging, let him encourage. Love must be sincere.
Hate what is evil; cling to what is good. Be devoted to one another in brotherly love.
Honor one another above yourselves. Be joyful in hope, patient in affliction, faithful in prayer.
Rejoice with those who rejoice; mourn with those who mourn."

—Romans 12:6, 8, 9–10, 12, 15

Early on in my infertility journey a friend called me.

With a shaky voice, filled with emotion, she spoke.

"Now don't say anything until I'm through. I just want to tell you that I hate that you have to go through this. You would be a great mother and it just makes me so angry that it's not happening! I just don't understand it at all. OK, that's all I had to say."

Whoa!

She acknowledged my pain and felt it with me. She didn't offer any empty advice or spiritual Band

Aids®. She expressed love to me and showed her emotions. That was a tremendous source of comfort to me.

I often think of her words in times of infertility heartache. They still make me smile.

Pick up the phone!

Bearing Fruit

Do you know someone who's going through a difficult time? Pick up the phone to say you are hurting for him or her. Ask how you can pray.

Day Seventy-Five

What My Best Friend Does Right

"As iron sharpens iron, so one man sharpens another."

—Proverbs 27:17

- She is sensitive to me.
- She cries with me about it.
- She laughs with me about it.
- She never pretends she can totally understand.
- She loves me through it.
- She's said she "wished she could fix it."
- She told me it wasn't fair.
- She told me I would be an amazing Mommy.
- She rejoiced over her daughter's pregnancy, but also thought of me.
- She faithfully loves me through it.
- She asks questions.
- She stands by me through hard times.
- She holds me when I cry.
- She is sensitive to comments others make and to the issue of infertility.
- She tenderly loves me through it.
- She advocates my cause.

- She shares the love of her grandchildren with me.
- She wrestles through tough issues with me.
- She doesn't baby me when I feel sorry for myself and wallow in self-pity.
- She courageously loves me through it.
- She spends sleepless nights wrestling in prayer for me.
- She is careful to ask me if it's uncomfortable to discuss some things.
- She lets me vent without judging me.
- She doesn't give me empty platitudes.
- She constantly loves me through it.
- She lets me talk about it.
- She has cried many tears because of my pain.
- She encourages me to take action, appropriately and carefully.
- She often has no words, just a hug, sharing my burden.
- She sacrificially loves me through it.
- She holds my hand and prays for me before surgeries…and brings gifts.
- She exhorts me to embrace my pain.
- She compels me to grasp what God is teaching through my pain.
- She encourages me to share what I'm learning with others.

- She inspires me to write out my thoughts.
- She never fails to love me through it.

Bearing Fruit

Make a list of the things your family or friends do right for you to help you through the pain of infertility. Show them the list and thank them.

Day Seventy-Six

Focus of Love

"Now that you have purified yourselves by
obeying the truth
so that you have sincere love for your brother,
love one another deeply, from the heart."

—I Peter 1:22

I try to avoid the baby section at the store. All the items seem to mock me. My heart shrivels when I see the little clothes and socks and bibs.

But one particular day I had to enter the baby section. I wanted to get a gift for my friend's new granddaughter. Hesitant at first, I gained courage with each step.

Well, let my friend explain it:

Focus of Love

by Gail Benn

I see you there,
timid, fearful, full of pain…
racked with grief and years of emotion,
—unspent…
wanting to love, yet wanting to run,
to hide…
to bury the burden of your heart.

Yet with the strength of love,
you moved…
ever so slowly,
building confidence with each step,
God embracing your pain-filled heart,
with His pain, His sacrifice, His love.
Love moves us, motivates, and completes.
God is love.

Your focus of love moved you,
beyond the barrier of pain…
to *God-confidence.*
He—bearing your burden,
as you kept in step with Him—
motivated by Love.

The joy of giving filled your heart,
'til there was no room
for pain's mastery.
Love's filling crumbled pain's walls.

Can't you see the Cross?
His love crumbled death's hold,
and gave freedom.

Bearing Fruit

Ah yes, I experienced a great freedom that day. The cold reality is that those in your sphere of life will continue to have babies. Look to God for courage in getting past the pain in order to celebrate the joy of others. It's not easy, but it's well worth it: freedom!

Day Seventy-Seven

Celebrate Freedom

"It is for freedom that Christ has set us free. Stand firm, then, and do not let yourselves be burdened again by a yoke of slavery."

—Galatians 5:1

Infertility has shackled me. I cannot seem to take a step without the burden of infertility dragging me down. I feel like I'm marked, cursed, and branded as *infertile*.

I cannot celebrate the news of a pregnancy without the reminder of my own personal inadequacy. People are awkward around me. I imagine whispers of pity for the barren one. I fear and obsess over what others might be saying about me. I am imprisoned by the breakdown of my womb.

Wretched woman that I am, who will rescue me from this body of death?

The Lord Jesus gently reminds me that I am *free*. It is for freedom that Christ has set me free. I will stand firm, then, and not let myself be burdened by a yoke of slavery. Casting off the shackles of Satan's lies, I exalt in the freedom Christ has obtained for me. I will no longer be bound by fears of what others might be saying or thinking. I will celebrate freely the joys of the miracle of God's giving life within another woman's womb. Celebrate freedom—*exhilarating, God-given freedom!*

I rest in His redemption. I celebrate life!

Bearing Fruit

Jesus' death on the Cross was for our freedom. We can have victory over any sin because of Him. Recognize Satan's lies when they come at you. Cast off the shackles of sin and enjoy freedom. Ask Jesus to take away your sin now. Accept His sacrifice. Break free!

Day Seventy-Eight

Shared Pain

"But God sent me ahead of you to preserve for you a remnant on earth and to save your lives by a great deliverance. So then, it was not you who sent me here, but God."

—Genesis 45:7–8

There I was, visiting my friend's church. I was dismayed to read in the church bulletin that it was "Baby Dedication Sunday," and the sermon was on Psalm 127.

Oh great, the ever popular, "You are so richly blessed if your quiver is chock full of kids." I wondered why *I* was there.

I felt my sprit sag as I hunched down in the pew. My friend, knowing full well that the wound of infertility was about to be sliced open, leaned over and spoke to me.

"Why don't you refocus and pray for that couple in the second row?" she said. "They are in the same pain as you are."

I did just that.

The sermon was difficult. There was no malicious intent on the pastor's part, yet not one word of compassion was offered to those without children. After the sermon, however, it became clear why I was there.

My friend and I were saddened to see the heart-broken couple in the second row. The sermon had devastated them. Tears streamed down the woman's cheeks. Her husband had an anguished look on his face. *Isn't church supposed to be a safe haven, a place of healing for the soul?*

My friend introduced me to the couple as "one who shared their pain." I looked at the crying woman and couldn't say a word, but we took hands and our eyes searched deep for comfort from each other. I understood her pain so perfectly. She suggested we pray.

So, the couple, a few of their friends, my friend, and I, huddled together to seek solace in our Lord. Strength was found and comfort was poured out.

I had no doubt in my mind that the Lord in all His sovereignty had brought me there for His purpose.

Bearing Fruit

Be prepared to minister to your fellow infertiles. Your own heart will be strengthened as you refocus and seek grace to comfort someone else. God gives pain purpose.

Day Seventy-Nine

Only God

"Do not grieve, for the joy of the Lord is your strength."

—Nehemiah 8:10

God's provision has been evident to me on a daily basis. He has put a joy in my heart, despite constant reminders of my infertility.

Only God could give me the strength to smile when I hear a child's giggle.

Only God could give me the strength to hold someone else's baby and enjoy it without feeling empty.

Only God could give me strength to get a gift for someone else's newborn.

Only God could give me strength not to break down in sobs at a commercial showing a mother cuddling her baby.

Only God could give me strength not to feel guilty that *I* am probably the reason we haven't been able to have children.

Only God could give me strength to laugh and to cry and to keep on living.

Only God's sufficient grace can give me that joy, that strength.

And so I go *from strength to strength,* assured that when I come to a point of weakness, *He* will provide the strength—and carry me through that time.

Bearing Fruit

A tremendous amount of strength is needed for an infertile couple to face a world full of children. You're stronger than you think. And when you falter, only God can get you through—only God.

Day Eighty

The Essence of Who I Am

"O Lord, you have searched me and you know me. If I rise on the wings of the dawn, if I settle on the far side of the sea, even there your hand will guide me, your right hand will hold me fast. I praise you because I am fearfully and wonderfully made; your works are wonderful, I know that full well. All the days ordained for me were written in your book before one of them came to be. Search me, O God, and know my heart."

—Psalm 139:1, 9–10, 14, 16, 23

I bitterly cried to my friend.

An HSG test supposedly showed some serious defects in my reproductive organs. (This later proved to be a false alarm.) I wearily asked her why God would allow the desire to bear children to remain if all along He knew it would be physically impossible for me. Why couldn't this have been discovered long ago—before I would dream of being a mother?

My friend's reply stopped my bitter complaints right in their tracks.

She stated that if I had known all along that I was unable to bear children, I might have closed myself off from the love of children. I might have protected my heart from reaching out to them if I had known I would never have my own.

Therefore, I would've been a far different woman than I am. I would not have the rapport and magnetism I now enjoy with children. I would not have the many, many children in my life who love me dearly. Indeed, the very core of my personality, my character, would be altered.

No, she insisted, God planted that desire for children with a higher purpose in mind: to mold me into the very essence of who I am.

Bearing Fruit

It may seem as though it would've been easier had you known all along that you would never have children. But all of our experiences, as well as desires, mold us into what we become. Think of how you would've been had you known about your infertile future. Many things could've turned out differently—even negatively. Praise Him, for you are fearfully and wonderfully made!

PART FIVE

Magnified Trust: How God is Sovereign Even in Our Suffering

"Hannah went on to testify that God was in the business of turning emptiness into fullness, sadness into joy, longing into satisfaction. Hannah found her source of joy in her Lord, not in her child."

— Cindy Lewis Dake,
from *Infertility: A Survival Guide for Couples and Those Who Love Them*

"My heart rejoices in the Lord; in the Lord my horn is lifted high.
There is no one holy like the Lord; there is no one besides you; there is no Rock like our God."

—I Samuel 2:1, 2

Scripture clearly shows God's sovereignty and trustworthiness in the darkest of times. Suffering is a gift. That's a concept that takes much maturity and spiritual growth to grasp and believe. If the childless woman cannot trust God, she will find herself to be quite bitter.

Day Eighty-One

Purpose in Pain

"Have mercy on me, O God, have mercy on me,
for in you my soul takes refuge.
I will take refuge in the shadow of your wings
until the disaster has passed.
I cry out to God Most High, to God, who fulfills
his purpose for me.
He sends from heaven and saves me, rebuking
those who hotly pursue me;
God sends his love and his faithfulness."

—Psalm 57:1–3

S*o, does God have a purpose in my infertility?* I considered that question…with more questions.

Is there purpose in a fire destroying a home? Is there purpose in a spouse dying in a car accident? Is there purpose in a child being sexually abused? Is there purpose in a diagnosis of cancer? Is there purpose in an elderly person living out the end of their years with Alzheimer's?

I don't see a purpose in any of it! None of it makes any sense to me!

Yet there is purpose in the pain.

In and of itself, infertility doesn't make or break me. Any of the painful realities of life could lead me to the same purpose. That is, finding purpose in my pain. The vehicle of pain is not what matters.

But, when I look at the pain, I see the path of purpose.

This pain has led me to a deeper trust of God. This pain has led me to comfort others. This pain has led me to write out my thoughts to share with others. This pain continues to reveal purpose in itself. It leads me to the only perfect comfort available—the everlasting arms of a kind and loving Lord Jesus. That is His purpose fulfilled for me!

Bearing Fruit

It's an exercise in futility trying to figure out why you're infertile. You'll never find an answer in this life. Instead, look for purpose in the pain. Where has this pain given purpose? May you feel amazement at how God has fulfilled His purpose.

Day Eighty-Two

I Saw the Lord

"In the year that King Uzziah died, I saw the Lord seated on a throne,
high and exalted, and the train of his robe filled the temple.
Then I heard the voice of the Lord saying,
'Whom shall I send? And who will go for us?' And I said, 'Here am I. Send me.'"

—Isaiah 6:1, 8

Lord, why is this? Why no children for us? This is too hard. It's too painful.

Every day sends a reminder. Walking through life infertile—it's gut-wrenchingly difficult.

We mourn the loss of a child that never was, nor ever will be. Tears flow. Despair, loneliness, sleepless nights…it seems like no one understands this pain. *How will we ever make it through?*

The Lord, in all His holiness, bent down and answered me.

"That's the way things are, but this is Who I AM: the 'Alpha and Omega,' the 'Creator of all Things,' the 'Mighty God,' the 'Everlasting Father,' the 'King of Kings,' the 'Lord of Lords,' the 'Judge,' the 'Redeemer,' the 'Bread of Life,' the 'Light of the World,' the 'Good Shepherd,' the 'Resurrection and the Life,' the 'Way, the Truth, and the Life,' the 'Almighty God,' the 'Living One, full of Grace and Compassion and Mercy,' the 'Majestic One' and holy, holy, holy, 'Abba Father.' I AM that I AM."

I fell to my knees.

Then I rose with the strength given to me by the "Great I Am."

Here am I, Lord, send me! I rise, ready.

Bearing Fruit

Walking through life infertile requires much time spent on our knees in prayer. When Isaiah caught sight of the holiness and majesty of the Lord, he was overcome. This same holy and majestic Lord still asks, "Whom shall I send?" Look away from your desperate circumstances and look instead to the character of God. He promises to strengthen you to face anything. Will you go?

Day Eighty-Three

Take the Cup

"'Abba Father,' He said, 'everything is possible for you. Take this cup from me. Yet not what I will, but what you will.'"

—Mark 14:36

On the worst night of His life Jesus prays that His Father would take the cup away. He is facing a grisly death by Crucifixion. He is sinless, but is about to take the sins of the entire world upon Himself. Worst of all, He will face isolation from His Father.

In agony He asks if there might be another way to save sinners. But God is silent. There *is* no other way. God does not take away the cup, but He does strengthen His Son to receive it.

God could choose to take this cup of infertility from me I think. I know I did not take the cup of my own will. It was handed to me. I would *never* have chosen this cup. Everything in me has wanted a child. There was no question in my heart, no hesitation, no absence of longing....

Please, this is not what I planned at all.

Please, this is too bitter to swallow.

Sometimes I would rather give up than face the daily struggle of infertility. That's how much it hurts some days.

And yet, the cup remains in my hands. The Lord gently bids me drink in trust. *Not what I will, but what my Sovereign Lord wills....*

As the Lord Jesus trusted Abba Father, I too will obediently bring the cup to my lips.

Bearing Fruit

Though you will never face the magnitude of what the Lord Jesus faced before going to the Cross, you can still get a limited sense of Gethsemane as you face trials. You can be obedient through your circumstances. The Holy Spirit will minister to you, giving you the supernatural strength to drink the cup of infertility.

Day Eighty-Four

Trust! Trust! Trust!

"You will keep in perfect peace him whose mind is steadfast, because he trusts in you. Trust in the Lord forever, for the Lord, the Lord, is the Rock eternal."

—Isaiah 26:3–4

I must keep focused. Focused on the Lord…the "Rock eternal."

Yet still, my mind is on a baby. It always is when I am wondering if I could possibly be pregnant. I constantly need to remind myself to trust in His timing. My weak flesh says, *Now! Why not now? It must be now.*

But my spirit says: *Trust. Always trust.*

I fight to focus my thoughts. I feel rushed, uncertain, hesitant, afraid, and disjointed. My thoughts scatter in all directions but I let them come to rest on God. With every step I listen for His Voice, though it be a mere whisper.

It is so easy to lose my focus. It is so easy to question God's sovereignty in subtle ways. It is so easy to worship at the altar of fertility. But I will find perfect peace when I steadfastly focus on God and renew my trust in Him. I will let my spirit's cry drown out the constant questions and confusion.

Trust! Trust! Trust!

Bearing Fruit

Let this be your battle cry when you must fight encroaching thoughts that threaten your peace of mind. Trust! Trust! Trust! Keeping a steadfast mind is one of the most difficult things in facing any trial. And infertility can be a long, drawn out struggle. The Holy Spirit will urge you on: Trust! Trust! Trust!

Day Eighty-Five

"Under Sovereign Management"

"His compassions never fail. They are new every morning; great is your faithfulness. The Lord is my portion; therefore I will wait for him."

—Lamentations 3:22–24

Abba Daddy is faithful, kind, gracious, abounding in love, forgiving, and compassionate. He is wisdom and love. He is the perfect timekeeper.

Forgive me that I presume to know better. My small mind contains small answers. My finite vision thinks I see all, when I see only to the end of my nose.

It's about perspective. I see only my poor, sad soul. He sees all. *Why is it so hard for me to trust the Creator of the Universe?*

Hannah Whitall Smith says: "It is not hard, you find, to trust the management of the universe, and all the outward creation, to the Lord. Can your case then be so much more complex and difficult than these, that you need to be anxious or troubled about His management of you?"

Every morning He brings on more blessings. *Bring them on, Lord!* I find comfort in the simple fact that I don't have to solve the problem of gravity each morning before I put one foot in front of the other. And, for that matter, I don't even have to recall how to work these feet; they just work.

By the same token, the Creator and Manager of the Universe is also the Creator and Manager of my womb. He is faithful and compassionate. I can cast aside my anxiety and know that my little world spins according to His great Hand.

Bearing Fruit

Crack open a science book or search the Internet for scientific marvels. Tune into the "Discovery Channel" or a *National Geographic* television special. *There's no end to the wonders of creation! Marvel too that you are on intimate terms with the magnificent Lord and Creator of all things. He can manage you. Be gone, anxiety!*

Day Eighty-Six

Jumping through Hoops

"I will guide you in the way of wisdom and lead you along straight paths.
When you walk, your steps will not be hampered, when you run, you will not stumble.
Hold on to instruction, do not let it go; guard it well, for it is your life."

—Proverbs 4:11–13

I fall into the trap of believing that if I do this, this, and that, then I will get pregnant. If I learn to control my temper, if I study God's Word every day, and spend one hour on my knees every morning at 5:00 A.M., then I will get pregnant. If I pursue a full-time job, if my husband gets promoted, *if…if…if….*

The list goes on and on. I drive myself at a frantic pace, scrolling through a flurry of "answers" and feverishly searching for the right combination. I try to convince myself that if I jump through the "right" hoops or "enough" hoops, then God will allow the pregnancy for which I've been praying.

But God is not a supernatural ringmaster, cracking His whip, forcing us to perform tricks for a cosmic audience of angels. We are not trapped animals performing the "Childless Couples' Barren and Waiting Circus." If I don't perform a certain thing at a certain time in a certain way, it doesn't mean that God is withholding from me.

It took some time for me to refrain from *hoop-jumping* and instead rely on the instruction of my heart by my loving Lord. He has promised to guide by instruction. That instruction is found in the Bible.

Pray to see God's character accurately.

Bearing Fruit

There is absolutely no magic number of hoops to jump through in order to get pregnant. God is not waiting for you to do this or that. If it seems that this is the "right time" for it to happen, it probably won't. It's horrible to ride that roller coaster of futile fertile hopes! God guides you gently to His will. He doesn't make you perform first. Dig into a Bible study *on getting through pain. A good one is called* Living with Infertility, *by Robin and Roger Sonneberg.*

Day Eighty-Seven

Faith like Abraham

"Abram said, 'O Sovereign Lord, what can you give me since I remain childless? Then the Lord said, 'Look up at the heavens and count the stars—if indeed you can count them… so shall your offspring be,' Abram believed the Lord."

—Genesis 15:2, 5–6

Abraham walked by faith. *That was all he had.*

He had God's promise, but he could've chosen not to trust God. No big deal. In that case, God would've chosen another to be the father of many nations. But Abraham had faith in God's promise. He obeyed God. Not *perfectly*, but he obeyed.

Abraham had the promise of a son. God certainly took His time in fulfilling that promise, but it was right on schedule by His timetable.

Abraham and Sarah may have had a tougher time waiting because they were given the promise of countless offspring. Yet years went by and the biological clock was so old it stopped ticking! Nevertheless, Abraham still "believed God."

I want to have faith like Abraham. Like him, I will walk by faith and believe the Lord.

I have a mother's heart. I fully trust that if God does not give me my own child, He will fulfill the purpose of my mother's heart in His way.

Bearing Fruit

Explore other outlets for your mother's heart. Spend time with nephews and nieces. Tutor at a school, teach a Sunday School class.... Open your heart to a need that exists in your world.

Day Eighty-Eight

Eyes on the Lord

"Good and upright is the Lord. He guides the humble in what is right. My eyes are ever on the Lord."

—Psalm 25:8, 9, 15

Sometimes my faith is like my physical eyesight—weak. I need corrective lenses to see clearly.

Similarly, I need the Lord to correct my spiritual weakness so that I may believe with greater clarity. I trust that my way is not cloudy or dim, but that my way is clear to see and perform His will.

Now, often this is only a temporary measure. When I take out my contact lenses, I no longer see clearly. When I look away from God's Spirit, I no longer see with spiritual clarity.

This is going to sound wacky, but bear with me. I recently had Lasik surgery to alleviate my need to wear contacts at all. My clear vision is no longer temporary, but permanent. I was thrilled to finally have a surgery that corrected something. After other surgeries to "correct" my infertility problem, all to no avail, this was a great relief! But I digress.

I need "spiritual laser vision" in order to keep my eyes on the Lord—a powerful and pinpoint focus straight to the truth. That way any insight gained can be permanent, not temporary.

My eyes are ever on the Lord.

Bearing Fruit

Consider the power of lasers. If only you could have laser sight to see God! Well, you can. Keep in His word and keep praying. Don't get distracted by temporary fixes. Keep your eyes on Him.

Day Eighty-Nine

Wisdom

"If any of you lacks wisdom, he should ask God, who gives generously to all without finding fault, and it will be given to him. But when he asks, he must believe and not doubt."

—James 1:5–6

God is generous and worthy to be praised. He cares for every little need of His children. He is mercy, wisdom, goodness, and love. The Lord is to be exalted because He perfectly displays all wisdom. My "wisdom" next to His wisdom is nothing. His wisdom fills the universe. He knows what I need before I ask. He has already made provision. He has already made a way. He says, *"If any of you lacks wisdom, he should ask God."* So I do.

John Ortberg writes in *The Life You've Always Wanted*:

> God's purpose in guidance is not to get us to perform the right actions. His purpose is to help us become the right kind of people. Personhood is formed through making decisions. We learn to think and weigh options, we discover what we truly value, we take responsibility for our choices.

This infertility puzzle is mind-boggling, with a myriad of mazes. Only a perfect, holy God can lead me through them. As I ask, acknowledge Him, and follow, He guides me in decisions and builds wisdom within me.

Bearing Fruit

Seek God's wisdom. Dig into the Book of Proverbs and discover a wealth of wisdom. In seeking His wisdom, get knowledge to choose wisely. If knowledge is power (as the saying goes), God's wisdom is all-powerful—the perfect combination in making tough decisions.

Day Ninety

Trusting

"How long, O Lord? Will you forget me forever? How long will you hide your face from me? How long must I wrestle with my thoughts and every day have sorrow in my heart? But I trust in your unfailing love."

—Psalm 13:1–2, 5

How can I follow what I don't know?

How can I obey what You don't convey?

Why do You conceal what I need You to reveal?

Why do You stay silent when I need You to relent?

Is *no answer* an answer?

Is Your will so deeply hidden?

Am I not diligent to seek with all my soul and strength?

What must I do to be content?

Trust. Always trust. *I must trust.*

Bearing Fruit

How many times have you said, "If only I had the promise of a child, I could endure the wait?" Reconfigure your thinking to "trust mode." That's like putting your mind on cruise control. You just maintain current speed and take your foot off the pedal. Trusting God means you turn the driving over to Him. You don't even know the destination. You'll never be assured of anything in the future, so trust is all you've got. You might as well get good at it.

Day Ninety-One

"Dispel My Doubts."

"Trust in the Lord with all your heart and lean not on your own understanding; in all your ways acknowledge him, and he will make your paths straight."

—Proverbs 3:5–6

Theologian Oswald Chambers asked the searching question: "Have we come to the point where God can withdraw His blessings from us without our trust in Him being affected?"

Whoa. Loaded question. Is it not easy to trust when all is well? Life is calm and my faith rests easy by the babbling brook of abounding blessings. *But, wait, what's this?* Unexpected and difficult circumstances. *No child? But that was my dream!*

Why would God refuse to bless my womb? Do I trust Him about this? Well, of course I, um, well…I want to trust…but this pain makes it difficult. Why would He not bless me this way? It makes no sense to me.

God does not promise to give a child to each of us, but He does promise to give peace to all of His children. I want to trust Him. Trust can be elusive since it is not an act of doing but a state of being.

His grace is sufficient. He is enough for me. *Do I believe that?* I am slowly beginning to....

With a trembling hand I reach for Your Grace. One drop is given.

Surely, it cannot be enough, Lord! I need much more!

"My grace is sufficient."

Lord, I trust You. Please dispel my doubts with your sufficient grace.

Bearing Fruit

Be honest with yourself and acknowledge it if you question God's wisdom in your childlessness. It's not about understanding; it's about trust. You'll never understand this side of heaven. Ask for the grace to trust Him more.

Day Ninety-Two

Wrestling in Prayer

"How long must I wrestle with my thoughts and every day have sorrow in my heart? But I trust in your unfailing love."

—Psalm 13:2, 5

Time and time again I have wrestled with God over my infertility. And, time and time again, God reminds me to *rest in Him* rather than fight. He wants me to stop struggling and simply to trust Him. I want to trust, but trust leaks out of my broken heart.

Sorrow floods my heart and overcomes the hope that trust gives. I watch it pour out of me, and I'm helpless to stop it. I continue to struggle.

Eventually I am driven to my knees. The Lord strengthens me with His unfailing love. It is futile to fight. *It certainly doesn't bring me a baby.*

The empowerment of my loving Lord binds up my broken heart and fills it with the hope that only He can provide.

Bearing Fruit

Wrestle with God in prayer. When He comforts, receive it. When you hear that still, small Voice speak gently to your heart, allow it to quiet your soul. You cannot change anything by struggling against it, but you can release frustration in fervent prayer. Give yourself focused time to do so. His love will not fail you.

Day Ninety-Three

The Infertility Marathon

"Commit your way to the Lord; trust in Him. If the Lord delights in a man's way,
He makes his steps firm; through he stumble, he will not fall,
for the Lord upholds him with His hand.
Wait for the Lord and keep His way."

—Psalm 37:5, 23–24, 34

I learned a lot about trusting God when I ran.

In running, you need endurance and determination. It doesn't come easily. You've got to train. And train. And train. You've got to have a goal or you won't have the desire to keep going.

When I first started running my friend and I set a goal to participate in a five-mile run. We trained for about seven months. I never expected to run four-minute miles, but I expected to finish the race.

Well, I finished—just ahead of the police car trying to allow traffic back on the race route. Sure, I finished, but not before I nearly gave up, wanting to simply sit down and say, "Forget it!"

Yes, I finished, despite the fact that I hated practically every minute of that run.

This infertility journey may be a long one. I will probably want to give up. I may hate every minute. Indeed it is the Infertility Marathon. To run well and to finish, it is vital I stay hydrated with *Living Water.* Stay focused. Stay steady, steady, *steady.*

Stay "in pursuit of trust."

Bearing Fruit

Physical exercise of some level is important for everyone, but it can be an integral part in helping to combat the stress of infertility. Set a daily goal of physical activity and let it teach you about trusting God.

Day Ninety-Four

9-11

"For the time will come when you will say,
'Blessed are the barren women, the wombs that never bore, and the breasts that never nursed.'
Then they will say to the mountains,
'Fall on us!' and to the hills, 'Cover us.'"

—Luke 23:29–30

September 11, 2001.

That date causes a stir in the heart of every American. The historic day's emotions have subsided, but the memories from the first airplane crash to the unbelievable unfolding of events that followed will forever stand bold in our minds.

September 11, 2001.

That was a day parents held their children a little tighter; they took a little extra time to tuck them in that night.

It was a day the worry factor of every parent shot up 100%.

It was a day when the joy of pregnancy was tainted by the loss of dear ones.

That was a day fear replaced excitement at the thought of a new life coming into this world.

That was a day when the barren women felt blessed.

Bearing Fruit

Much has been and will be written or said about that mind-numbing day: September 11, 2001. What were your feelings that day? Did you consider the blessing of barrenness? I'm sure Jesus speaks of a far greater horror in the Luke passage, but I understood the blessing of barrenness in a different way on that day.

Day Ninety-Five

Empty Quiver

"Sons are a heritage from the Lord; children a reward from Him.
Like arrows in the hands of a warrior are sons born in one's youth.
Blessed is the man whose quiver is full of them."

—Psalm 127:3–5

Anger permeated my being as I sat through the sermon at a church I was visiting.

The teaching was that children are your heritage, your future, and the reward for your hard work. I had to pound down the pain with prayer. Respectfully, pastor, I must disagree. If you have children, indeed you must look at them in that light, but because God has not given me children, this does not stamp a huge "cursed" on my forehead. My empty quiver does not reveal that I am not a hard worker. This does not mean I have no heritage, no future, and no purpose.

Please, pastor, look out at your congregation. There are those who sit there hurting because of infertility; there are those who are single who have no children. Those words had to sting them a bit. What about those who have lost children to death? Was their reward taken away? Were they being punished?

I do not know why God has not given me children. But I'll tell you what I do know with full and complete confidence—and not a stutter, not a question in my voice: I know I can trust in the almighty sovereignty of the Lord God, and I know that ultimately my heritage, my future, my reward is the Lord Himself.

Bearing Fruit

If your pastor unknowingly causes pain, make an appointment and express your hurt. Most likely, he will welcome your words. Be an "infertility ambassador."

Day Ninety-Six

Not a Punishment

"To You, O Lord, I lift up my soul; in you I trust, O my God.
Do not let me be put to shame, nor let my enemies triumph over me.
Show me your ways, O Lord, teach me your paths; guide me in your truth and teach me,
for you are my God, my Savior, and my hope is in you all day long."

—Psalm 25:1, 4–5

At times I creep along hesitant and uncertain as I seek the Lord's will for my life. It's not that I don't trust Him. After I have logged this many "trust miles," I would be a fool indeed to doubt Him. No, it's a hesitancy and an uncertainty that stems from self-doubt.

There are times when I believe the lie that my infertility is a punishment of some measure. I begin to doubt that I even *deserve* motherhood. This ultimately carries over into doubting that I could possibly know His will for my life when I clearly deserve His punishment.

I must get through the shameful lies of Satan, the enemy, and instead place my hope in God alone. Indeed, I dare not hope in myself because I do deserve punishment. Not the punishment of infertility, but eternal punishment. That's what my sins deserve. Yet, I have a great Savior—a Savior who is not punishing me with infertility, but is giving me hope!

Bearing Fruit

Infertility is not a punishment from God! Don't let your thought process spiral down into a negative sequence of lies. Thank God for a Savior who has taken the punishment for your sins. Thank God for a Savior who can give hope in the midst of infertility. Start a "Thanksgiving Journal" today.

Day Ninety-Seven

"What's Done is Done."

"For no matter how many promises God has made, they are 'Yes' in Christ. And so through him the 'Amen' is spoken by us to the glory of God. Now it is God who makes both us and you stand firm in Christ. He anointed us, set his seal of ownership on us, and put his Spirit in our hearts as a deposit, guaranteeing what is to come."

—2 Corinthians 1:20–22

What's done is done. No matter what I do, or don't do, it is settled. What God has for me will be given to me in Christ Jesus. Nothing I do, or don't do, will change that.

This is the gospel message in its beautiful simplicity. Because I have Christ I have everything. All promises find their fulfillment in Christ. I didn't earn heaven (I can't), and I'll never lose what Christ has given to me. I gave my life to Christ Jesus and He gives eternal life to me. The Holy Spirit guarantees this.

When my nephew was about five-years-old I explained to him how Jesus died on the Cross and then, after three days, He became alive again. My nephew was curious.

"Did He die again, then?"

"No," I explained, "He was the winner over death. And He is still alive."

That question from a child's mind bears a deeper theological truth. Jesus died *once* as a sacrifice for everyone's sin. And those who choose to die to their sins and accept that sacrifice *will* gain Jesus' Resurrection life, never to die again.

When I am troubled about my infertility it's like I die again. I allow the worry to overtake me and I wonder how I can stand against the pain. The Holy Spirit reminds me that God makes me stand firm in Christ!

And so, at times, I stop worrying and wondering—and instead I wait and watch. *What will God do? How will He do it? When will He do it?*

It's all in His hands. It's all under His sovereignty. All this worrying and wondering—*What's the good in it?*

I will wait and watch and see the way He works.

Now let my soul be settled in Christ.

Bearing Fruit

I wonder why we worry when worry really wearies. There's a tongue-twister for you to recite the next time you start worrying. "What's done is done." Worry accomplishes nothing. Do you have the assurance of eternal life? Only Jesus Christ's victory conquers the weight of worry. Stand firm in Him!

Day Ninety-Eight

Expectation

"Give ear to my words, O Lord, consider my sighing. Listen to my cry for help, my King and my God, for to you I pray. In the morning, O Lord, you hear my voice; in the morning I lay my requests before you and wait in expectation."

—Psalm 5:1–3

I must hear God today.

I struggle with the thought of having no children. I need help to maintain peace in His will, to rest in His sovereignty.

Hear my cry, O Lord!

Dare I ask again for God to give me a child? I'm pretty sure He's familiar with that request by now. I ask again. I ask for that little baby to care for and to love—to cuddle, to nurture, to protect, to teach, and to hold.

Hear my cry, O Lord!

I pour my heart out with this request.

But days go by, and then months, then years, and still no child.

I know the Lord has heard me. I continue to wait in expectation. Something will come of these requests. Something....

I wait in expectation for whatever it may be.

Bearing Fruit

God hears our voice of prayer. He hears our requests. Keep on praying. Something will come of it. It's different for each of us. Expect His help.

Day Ninety-Nine

Baby Dolls

"No one whose hope is in you will ever be put to shame, but they will be put to shame who are treacherous without excuse. Show me your ways, O Lord, teach me your paths; guide me in your truth and teach me, for you are God my Savior, and my hope is in you all day long."

—Psalm 25:3–5

Don't count your chickens before they hatch." This silly saying took on a different meaning when I applied it to having children.

Long before the wedding day it begins. Dreams of motherhood are clearly shown in the number of baby dolls nestled in the arms of little girls. When I see a sweet, darling little girl tenderly loving her dolly, I can't help but feel a certain sadness to think that that little girl may never bear a living, breathing baby to hold and nurture.

So what's the answer? Take away baby dolls? Take away dreams? Ingrain into a couple in premarital counseling not to count on children?

No way. Despite the pain I face daily, this would be far too cynical a solution.

Instead we should put our hopes and dreams into the hands of the sovereign Lord. Let Him take it from there. That doesn't mean we'll have our 2.5 children, but it does mean that our focus will be on what God is doing and our hope will remain in what He will do.

He will guide us along hopeful paths and through difficult circumstances. He promises that we will never be put to shame.

I'm all for dreams...and baby dolls, too.

Bearing Fruit

Buy a niece or a friend's daughter a baby doll. Let her dream.

PART SIX

Maximized Contentment: How God Promises Peace

"I have no doubt that [God] is able to give me a child; but without omniscience, I'm unconvinced that it's for my best. We have to wonder if what we're asking for, even believing God for, is actually what He considers best for us. God in His eternal wisdom is the One who determines whether or not to give us what we ask for. We have to recognize that our perspective is finite."

—Sandra Glahn, Th.M.,
and William Cutrer, M.D.,
from *When Empty Arms Become a Heavy Burden*

"I have fought the good fight, I have finished the race, I have kept the faith.
Now there is in store for me the crown of righteousness, which the Lord,
the righteous Judge, will award to me on that day."

—II Timothy 4:7–8

Can contentment be found even if our dream of having a child never comes to fruition? We can find it only through supernatural contentment, which can only come from divine peace. This section points the way to contentment—a happy ending, even if a child is never born to the infertile couple.

Day One Hundred

Constant and Trustworthy

"I know that you can do all things; no plan of yours can be thwarted.
You asked, 'Who is this that obscures my counsel without knowledge?'
Surely I spoke of things I did not understand, things too wonderful for me to know.
My ears had heard of you, but now my eyes have seen you."

—Job 42:2–3, 5

Sometimes the days drift lazily by, but mostly they fly by in a whirlwind of activity. Every day that passes seems a day lost, as it's another day I'm not pregnant. I often begrudge my infertile circumstances and look at them as the sum of my life. In reality, God has given so much, yet I have complained so much.

I don't have to be ruled by circumstances, nor can I rule them. I can respond in acceptance that my present circumstances are God's will.

By His Hand come hard times and by His Hand comes strength. By His Hand come mountains to climb and by His Hand comes endurance. By His Hand come sad times and by His Hand comes comfort. By His Hand come blessings and by His Hand comes grace.

I see my Lord in every part of my life. I take His Hand. He is constant and trustworthy.

Bearing Fruit

There is no getting around God's sovereignty. You can balk at it all you want, but God will not move. We will never understand why we suffer as we do. Do an in-depth study on the book of Job to get a better handle on God's sovereignty in the midst of suffering.

Day One Hundred One

Christ's Power

"There was given me a messenger of Satan, to torment me.
[The Lord's] power is made perfect in weakness.
Therefore I will boast all the more gladly about my weaknesses,
so that Christ's power may rest on me; for when I am weak, then I am strong."

—2 Corinthians 12:7, 9–10

As a believer in Jesus Christ I will never face the eternal fires of hell, but while I'm here on earth the sparks can sometimes reach my life and burn a place in my heart. In fact, these are the very messengers that Satan sends to torment me. They attack in various forms. That's the way it is this side of heaven. They attempt to make me feel small and inadequate, especially when they torment me with my infertility.

Infertility is a weakness. Often when in the throes of it, I have discovered weaknesses I didn't even know I had. They are usually pretty evident for the entire world to see—anger, in the absence of trust, sorrow, in the absence of faith....

Still, God's sovereignty stands. All my whining and cajoling and pouting and temper tantrums won't change anything. Satan's messengers taunt me all the more in those times.

How do I combat them? I beat them down with Christ's power! By the authority of His shed Blood these demons are pulverized, trivialized, terrorized into puny, cartoonish, clownish, simpering, whimpering nothings!

Christ's power and greatness are displayed magnificently when His love and strength gets me through, despite my not being blessed with a child. At those times, others may actually marvel at how much I trust Him.

Now that shows power!

Bearing Fruit

Have a battle plan ready so you can be prepared for Satan's attacks. The best defensive weapon available to us is God's Word. Volley Scripture verses such as 2 Corinthians 12:7–10 when caught in a firefight, and let Christ's power rest on you. Your weakness can be transformed into a mighty show of God's power. Think of that the next time you view fireworks. The magnificent display of beauty and light combined with thunderous noise is a symbolic picture of His mighty power. Ask the Lord to turn your weakness into a tremendous display of powerful fireworks!

Day One Hundred Two

The Beauty of Barrenness

"There is a time for everything, and a season for every activity under heaven."

—*Ecclesiastes 3:1*

Barrenness evokes a stark, empty feeling, a sense of nothingness. As we walked in the woods, my friend challenged me to a bolder and unconventional way of looking at barrenness.

In the forest that day, the leafless trees seem naked and severe. We are indoctrinated with the concept that beauty can be found only in the blossoms and foliage of fully adorned trees. With fresh eyes, my friend saw a far different perspective. To her, the barrenness of the trees made for aesthetically pleasant scenes in the striking, monochromatic shades of gray, brown, and green, with tiny hints of color. She pointed out the stately, almost mystical way we viewed each limb reaching heavenward.

"It's a mystery how this barren expression can become something so different as each season brings about change," she said, simply.

I considered this application to my barren womb. My barrenness can take on a beauty all its own in the hands of God. My infertility has caused me to reach heavenward, longing to accept His will. Each season has indeed brought change to my life as I have allowed the Master Painter to color the scenery.

Bearing Fruit

Take a walk in the late autumn woods and discover the beauty of barrenness. Behold the secret wisdom of God's mysterious seasons. Enjoy His magnificent creation.

Day One Hundred Three

Omni-Comforting

"Praise be to the God and Father of our Lord
Jesus Christ, the Father of compassion
and the God of all comfort, who comforts us in all
our troubles,
so that we can comfort those in any trouble with
the comfort we ourselves received from God."

—2 Corinthians 1:3–5

My church is generally sensitive to the childless on Mother's Day and Father's Day. I try to act as the "Sensitivity Police for the Infertile" on those days. I want to be sure they at least *mention us*.

But, at the service I attended this year there was no mention of the infertile ones. I sat in my pew, indignant, planning how on Monday I would speak to our pastor about this.

But then as I sat there scanning the faces of the choir members, the pastors, and various others, a simple thought came to me.

God seemed to say, "*Vicki, these people care about your pain, but they can't fill your needs all the time. Only I can comfort you constantly and to the depths that you need comforted. I care about you and I am all you need."*

While the Lord has put many loving and compassionate people in my life, the fact remains that there are limitations as to what I can ask of them. Only God is a consistent and constant Comforter, for only He is omnipresent.

This truth can translate into, "He is omnicomforting." His comfort is available to me at any time—and always in an unlimited supply.

Bearing Fruit

It takes guts for some to go to church on Mother's Day or Father's Day. Don't feel bad if there are times you just can't face it, especially if your church is not sensitive in this area. But if you go, know that the "Omni-Comforting One" is with you.

Day One Hundred Four

"Watch for Children"

"Where were you when I laid the earth's foundations? Tell me, if you understand.
Have you given orders to the morning, or shown the dawn its place?
What is the way to the abode of light? And where does darkness reside?
Then Job answered the Lord: 'I am unworthy—how can I reply to you?
I put my hand over my mouth.'"

—*Job 38:4, 12, 19; 40:3–4*

Even the street signs mock me.

"Watch for Children," they say.

Oh, I've watched for children, but they've never come to me. I've prayed about this for years, but God doesn't seem to be listening. My dreams sometimes involve children, but they are never my own children. This dream of children is an elusive one. This desire to be a mother is nothing but a mocking ache.

And at times I watch out for children so that I can close my eyes and not see them. I shield my eyes from them to protect myself. To see them is to feel the heartache of a blessing not given to me. Seeing children often fills me with despair. So I turn my head and shut my ears to their laughter.

I ask my Father in Heaven: *Must there be signs everywhere taunting me about my infertility?*

He always answers.

"Look beyond a physical sign. Look higher. Look up Here! Look at Me! Look at the wonders of My creation! Look at who I AM. . . ."

I put my hand over my mouth.

Bearing Fruit

Yes, even familiar street signs can bring a twinge of pain. You must move beyond the physical to find spiritual healing. Allow God's marvelous creation to astound you. Find joy in it. If you do, the complaining will stop and the hurt will fade.

Day One Hundred Five

Counter-Reproductive Organs

"For who knows what is good for a man in life, during the few and meaningless days he passes through like a shadow. When times are good, be happy; but when times are bad, consider: God has made the one as well as the other. Therefore, a man cannot discover anything about his future. Follow the ways of your heart and whatever your eyes see. So then, banish anxiety from your heart and cast off the troubles of your body."

—Ecclesiastes 6:12, 7:14, 11:9, 10

G*od knows my heart*. He knows I am weary. He sees my sagging spirit.

It exasperates me to see pregnancies come so easily to those who don't even want a child. To some who are not ready, to some who are not fit to be mothers.

And here I am with my counter-reproductive organs.

Hey God, apparently I have defective parts. Where's that warranty on motherhood? What does it say in the small print?

"Female reproductive organs do not guarantee a resulting baby. Please see specialist for details."

What does God want? What should I do? Am I missing something?

He leads me to His Word. I find strength there, peace there, answers there. That's "God's Lifetime Warranty," which never expires. Even upon death, I cash in on the *eternal rewards* of believing without seeing. That's the Holy Spirit's guarantee.

Bearing Fruit

Say it out loud: "It's unfair." Admit these feelings to God. He understands.

Day One Hundred Six

Proud Mother of Forty Sons and Daughters

"And let not any eunuch complain, 'I am only a dry tree.' For this is what the Lord says: 'To the eunuchs who keep my Sabbaths, who choose what pleases me and hold fast to my covenant—to them I will give within my temple and its walls a memorial and a name better than sons and daughters; I will give them an everlasting name that will not be cut off.'"

—Isaiah 56:3–5

In the middle of Central Park I stood before the senior high youth group. I was one of several youth leaders on a ministry trip to New York City. I took a breath and spoke with deep emotion.

"I've been so proud of you guys, watching you serve God so well," I said. "Some of you know my husband and I have not been able to have children. Let me tell you something. Tonight, I stand before you, feeling like the proud mother of forty sons and daughters."

The kids loved it. Some of the guys came up to me afterward and teasingly asked if they could call me "Mom." The girls came up with tears and hugs.

And I realized the blessing I was getting. Their mothers and fathers did not get to see their children in action. God had allowed *me* that honor. So I will not complain, "I am only a dry tree."

Though God has not given me my own children, He has given a memorial, a ministry that makes a mark in eternity. For a ten-day period I witnessed the very best those teens could put forth. I witnessed how God used them in spreading the gospel.

And for a ten-day period I experienced that lump-in-your-throat-pride a parent feels as he or she experiences the successes of a child.

Bearing Fruit

Want an exhilarating challenge? Work with the teens at your church. It's a perfect way to get a taste of the teen world without having to live in it.

Day
One Hundred Seven

Infertility Rap

"I am the Alpha and Omega, the First and the Last, the Beginning and the End."

—Revelation 21:13

Infertility is a world of endless abbreviations from ART to ZIFT (for more on this, please see the *Infertility Decoder* at the end of this book). So here's a little rap in "ABCs of Infertility" lingo:

When you're introduced,
to A-R-T,
you'll experience,
an H-S-G.

A laparoscopy,
is next in line;
a hysteroscopy,
at the same time.

All along the way,
your BBT,
Elect to inject,
The hCG.

Now I know my ABCs—
ABCs of Infertility!

Come face to face,
with FSH.
Run race to race,
with the LH.

Clomid, Lupron,
Pergonal;
been there, done that;
had a ball!

Now let's go crazy,
hormonally;
Think that you're feeling,
"Bipolar-y."

Now I know my ABCs—
ABCs of Infertility!

Seems you see your doc,
more than your spouse;
in the waiting room,
more than your house.

Oh, here we go now,
time for your guy,
as an A-I-H,
for an I-U-I.

With IVF choose,
G-I-F-T;

all the way to
Z-I-F-T.

Now I know my ABCs—
ABCs of Infertility!

If you still don't have your,
B-A-B-Y,
really makes you want,
To C-R-Y.

But all is not lost,
take it from me:
just grab some hope, girl,
with G-O-D!

Just look to Him,
and you will see,
He's holding you,
lovingly.

Now I know my ABCs—
ABCs of Infertility!

My rhymin' is done,
I hope you're laughin',
This roller coaster,
is startin' to happen.

So just get on board,
and take a ride;
sometimes you just laugh,
cuz' you can't hide.

Infertility,
has got you down?
Just "rap" it up and,
turn it a-round.

Now I know my ABCs—
ABCs of Infertility!

I've never heard so many abbreviations in all my life! Seems that, in the infertility business, they are in such a rush for you to get pregnant there's no time to pronounce the full name of the technique, and so they abbreviate it.

Just wanted to give you a laugh.

"Peace out."

Bearing Fruit

Jesus said He is the Alpha and the Omega, A to Z. In the midst of fertility mumbo jumbo, place your ultimate hope in Him. And don't forget to find the humor in this painful process; it's there. And laughter is good medicine.

Day One Hundred Eight

A Time to Give Up

"There is a time for everything, and a season for every activity under heaven: a time to be born and a time to die...a time to weep and a time to laugh, a time to mourn and a time to dance... a time to search and a time to give up."

—Ecclesiastes 3:1, 2, 4, 6

In working with an infertility specialist, he or she can have the tendency to move things along at breakneck speed. After all, the specialist's job is for you to get pregnant.

Ed and I seemed to be speeding headlong into a brick wall. I'd had surgery, inseminations, and now our doctor was ready for Lupron and GIFT.

We *weren't* ready!

When faced with many decisions to continue the multiple medical pursuits, we had to come to terms with our own timetable. I found comfort in knowing that there *was* a time recognized by God to give up; a season when giving up was the *right thing*, the thing ordained of Him.

Not so much that we gave up, *per se,* but rather, we let go. When at last we did, we both felt a confident resolve and a blessed relief.

When you feel you can no longer face the mounting bills, the endless appointments, the arduous medical intrusions, then there is no shame in surrendering. If in fact you are honestly seeking His will, trust that God is leading you. You too may find comfort in knowing there is "a time to give up."

Bearing Fruit

Set your own pace. Research and ask questions before barreling ahead with medical procedures. This is especially important when expenses begin to mount up. Set goals and a timetable with your doctor. Count the cost.

Day One Hundred Nine

I Felt You in My Heart

"We wait eagerly for our adoption as sons, the redemption of our bodies.
For in this hope we were saved. Who hopes for what he already has?
But if we hope for what we do not yet have, we wait for it patiently."

—Romans 8:23–25

Is there a child out there (maybe even yet unborn) that needs my husband and me?

Sometime back I made a vow that I would trust God through infertility. I stood on a little bridge in a park as I prayed, and the quietest thought came to me. It seemed that in the future I would bring a little child there and say, "This is where I first felt you in my heart."

Now when that quiet thought first came to me I paid it little mind because I knew I would trust God whether I got pregnant or not. Now that it seems we will not conceive our own child, I ponder if it wasn't in fact a potential thought for an adopted child.

Perhaps God has chosen me to care for a "parent-less" child.

He has adopted me *through His Spirit. He has given me hope. I can give hope to a child longing for a home. I must consider prayerfully this high call since it may be that God is tugging at my heart.*

Bearing Fruit

If you are both ready to consider adoption, start asking around for information and begin researching options. Remember, adoption is not a cure for infertility, but a way to become a parent. Read Patricia Irwin Johnson's great book, Adopting after Infertility. *Perhaps God has chosen a child just for you. Infertility has made you wait. Start searching; a little one may be waiting for you.*

Day One Hundred Ten

Four Roads Diverge

"Although the Lord gives you the bread of adversity and the water of affliction, your teachers will be hidden no more; with your own eyes you will see them. Whether you turn to the right or to the left, your ears will hear a voice behind you, saying, 'This is the way; walk in it.'"

—Isaiah 30:20–21

Four roads diverge in the middle of this barren wood.

I consider the paths before me: Remain childfree? Adopt? Pursue aggressively through medical means? Wait?

Sometimes being childfree does not seem so bad. I consider the quiet moments, the freedom and the financial abundance.

Oh, but to adopt. . . . After we've been waiting so long for a child, I wonder if a child is somewhere waiting for us.

The medical wonders available to us are astonishing. It is almost scary how they manipulate sperm and egg through highly technological means these days. I can't begin to understand how it works, but most of it seems a blessing to the many who become parents that way.

Wait? Well, that's a road I know well. I could travel that one with my eyes closed. That's generally the only way to travel that road because we never can see up ahead.

Four roads diverge in the middle of this barren wood. I took the one God pointed out for me. And that's made all the difference.

Bearing Fruit

I can't stress enough the importance of getting all the information you can in order to make wise decisions. Get knowledge and wisdom. God will lead you.

Day One Hundred Eleven

Secret of Contentment

"I have learned to be content whatever the circumstances. I know what it is to be in need, and I know what it is to have plenty. I have learned the secret of being content in any and every situation. I can do everything through him who gives me strength."

—Philippians 4:11–13

What is the secret of contentment?

Infertility is a merciless thief. It robs so much from me. I feel depleted in so many ways. And as I approach each phase of life, a new emotion of what I am lacking crops up. The baby showers, school programs, graduations, weddings, grandchildren. As I age, each milestone absent from my life will tap me on the shoulder to remind me of what I do not have.

So how will I ever be content?

Paul reveals the secret.

First, it is *acceptance*. There has to be a decision to accept circumstances as they are. *What choice do I have?*

Secondly and key is to know that: *I can face anything with Christ who gives me His strength. He is faithful and only in Him will I find contentment.*

I doubt that the pain ever completely goes away, but there can be fulfillment and peace despite childlessness.

Remember this secret of contentment: *Strength is found in Christ and in Christ alone.*

Bearing Fruit

Yes, it gets easier. I know because it has for me—but only because of Christ. Without His strength, it's hopeless. Now you know the secret of contentment.

Day One Hundred Twelve

Leech's Daughter

"The leech has two daughters, 'Give! Give!' they cry. There are three things that are never satisfied, four that never say, 'Enough!': the grave, the barren womb, land, which is never satisfied with water, and fire, which never says, 'Enough.'"

—Proverbs 30:15–16

This verse doesn't give much hope for future contentment if we remain childless. A childless wife in ancient Israel was desolate, often desperate. In that day, a barren womb was a sign of God's curse. This is not true today. However, I can still relate to the concept of the unsatisfied womb.

In *When Empty Arms Become a Heavy Burden: Encouragement for Couples Facing Infertility* by Sandra Glahn and William Cutrer, M.D., this thought is put forth concerning the unsatisfied desire for a child: "To desire children is good, even the norm. Remember, Proverbs 30 reminds us that it's natural to long for children."

I cannot fight my longing for a child. Many people desire to have a child. Some are denied that fulfillment. It's not necessarily a negative thing if my womb never says, "Enough!"

So, is it hopeless? If my womb is never satisfied, am I forever to be a leech's daughter?

Not if I come to the place where God is enough. I will seek out the place in my infertility journey where I can say this: *God does indeed satisfy!*

Bearing Fruit

Read When Empty Arms Become a Heavy Burden *by Sandra Glahn and Dr. William Cutrer. This book encouraged me to begin my journey to find the place where God is enough.*

Day One Hundred Thirteen

Godly Offspring

"Has not the Lord made them one? In flesh and spirit they are his.
And why one? Because he was seeking godly offspring."

—Malachi 2:15

My husband and I have committed our marriage to the Lord. We long to reproduce a godly offspring to the Lord's honor and pleasure and grace. But thus far, the Lord is not seeking godly offspring from us. So, until that time would come (if ever), I am content in where I am now and in how I am now.

The Lord has given us the love of many children and I am grateful for that. He has asked that we tend to the godliness of many children. My husband and I faithfully taught kindergarten Sunday School for seven years. Recently I have taken on leadership with the senior high youth group. I take my role as a godly example before children and young people quite seriously.

We treasure the relationships we have with our nephew and nieces. We have close ties with them. I am grateful to my sister and brother-in-law for sharing the love of their children with us. It's a little slice of parenthood without the ultimate weight of responsibility. And Matthew and Heather and Emily are absolute angels! (Why do I hear their parents incredulously laughing?)

Despite the fact that we have not reproduced a biological godly offspring, we still are responsible to be godly and to have a part in the godliness—and lives— of children not our own. For that, I am most grateful.

In that, I feel productive.

Bearing Fruit

The absence of having your own children does not exempt you from responsibility as a role model before others. Take on the challenge to produce spiritual growth in a child; you will enjoy the fruits of it!

Day One Hundred Fourteen

Satisfaction

"My soul will be satisfied as with the richest of foods;
with singing lips my mouth will praise you.
My soul clings to you; your right hand upholds me."

—*Psalm 63: 5, 8*

I want a child of my own and yet I have been denied one. Though I have prayed that God would take my desire for a child away, I find it taps me on the shoulder time and time again.

This may seem like a trite example, but often I crave chocolate. *Do I need chocolate? No way! Will an apple taste just as good? No, but it will satisfy hunger just as well.*

I want a child. God gives many other blessings. *Will I still sometimes long for that child?* Of course, but the many other blessings He gives will satisfy, though in a different way.

Ultimately, God should be all that I need and want. He Is Satisfaction. I must ask my heart: *Is God sufficient?* I find that when I honestly seek Him to satisfy the longing of my heart, He does.

Lord, give me the spirit-sense to sort out my wants from my needs.

Bearing Fruit

Eat some chocolate and consider your blessings. List them and be amazed at how God has blessed you in such significant ways, despite not having children. Now, eat an apple. Tastes pretty good, huh?

Day One Hundred Fifteen

Dwell Where I Am

"The fruit of righteousness will be peace; the effect of righteousness will be quietness and confidence forever. My people will live in peaceful dwelling places, in secure homes, in undisturbed places of rest. How blessed you will be."

—Isaiah 32:17–20

My heart cries out for a child, but if a child were now to enter our lives, there would be drastic changes.

No more eating out twice, sometimes three times a week. No more spontaneous shopping. No more last-minute decisions to go to a movie. No more romantic interludes whenever, wherever we want. No more quiet times to myself in the evening. No more sports car. No more spending money with little thought. The list could go on.

Bottom line, everything would change, including our future.

As I consider all this, I find myself coming closer to contentment with things present. In fact, I've grown accustomed to our carefree and quiet lives. That doesn't mean I'm glad that we don't have children, but it does no good to dwell on and fret over what *could be*.

I will peacefully dwell where I am.

Bearing Fruit

My husband jokingly keeps a mental list of the benefits of not having children. You've got to admit, there are definite advantages. This is not to say you prefer it, but it's OK to enjoy the positives of your reality.

Day One Hundred Sixteen

Got My Sports Car

"Moreover, when God gives any man wealth and possessions, and enables him to enjoy them, to accept his lot and be happy in his work—this is the gift of God. A man may have a hundred children and live many years; yet no matter how long he lives, if he cannot enjoy his prosperity, this too is meaningless. Enjoy life with your wife, whom you love, all the days of this meaningless life that God has given you under the sun."

—Ecclesiastes 5:19; 6:3, 9; 9:9

Got my sports car!

My husband and I decided a few years back that if we didn't have a child soon, we would get sports cars.

We've got a surplus of money and a depletion of love—of a child to love, that is. Now I love my husband dearly. If I had to spend my life with *any* man, just we two, it would be this man. So there's no depletion of love that way.

He wanted me to have this sports car. In fact, he insisted that I get the new car even though it was *technically* his turn. He's been a phenomenal husband to have through this infertility journey. And our love grows deeper each day....

So, I've got a good-looking, loving husband, our cozy home with our sweet dog, loving family and friends, and an eternity to look forward to with the Lord Jesus Christ. Those are many excellent and amazing blessings.

Yes, I've got my sports car.

But there are days I'd trade it in for a family van, littered with toys and fast food wrappers, with little voices calling to *Mommy* and *Daddy.*

You, too?

Bearing Fruit

Get a sports car! OK, at least get yourself something you enjoy. It's alright to pamper yourself once in awhile.

Day One Hundred Seventeen

What about the Rest?

"Rejoice in the Lord always. I will say it again: Rejoice! Let your gentleness be evident to all. The Lord is near. Do not be anxious about anything, but in everything, by prayer and petition, with thanksgiving, present your requests to God. And the peace of God, which transcends all understanding, will guard your hearts and your minds in Christ Jesus.
Finally, brothers, whatever is true, whatever is noble, whatever is right, whatever is pure, whatever is lovely, whatever is admirable—if anything is excellent or praiseworthy—think about such things. And the God of peace will be with you."

—Philippians 4:4–9

What about the rest?

Resting…how do I rest?

Wait, there's no *doing* rest. You just… *rest.*

Not easy for someone who has been in the thick of infertility treatments month after month, when what you do could mean the difference between *having* and *not having* a child. Not that there's a 100 percent guarantee, but often treatment on some level *is* a prospective way to get pregnant.

What about the rest?

There comes a time in every childless woman's life when she must choose to rest. *OK, I choose it, now what?*

I take power naps. I lie down, close my eyes, and quickly drift into a light sleep for about fifteen minutes. I awake refreshed.

To rest in the Lord, try *power prayers.* When the anxiety or stress or depression starts to hit, pray. Pray what you're feeling. Let it flow. Don't hold back. Let the Lord hear your pain. He already knows about your pain, so you're not going to surprise Him with any negative thought you have. Power prayers help, and they work, too!

To rest in the Lord, try *power words.* Open the Bible and read until you are comforted. Psalms are a great place for power words. I don't have to read very long in the Psalms until some verse soothes my anxious soul. Go to your favorite verses. Read about how others faced adversity by resting in God. Power words help.

What about the rest?

The Lord Jesus suffered death on a Cross so that you could rest. *So just rest.*

Just rest.

Hush, now....

Bearing Fruit

Just got up from a refreshing power nap. We push our bodies too hard sometimes. We push our minds and emotions too hard. You need more power prayers and power words. Give yourself a rest.

Day One Hundred Eighteen

Tiny, Little Irony

"Forget the former things; do not dwell on the past. See, I am doing a new thing! Now it springs up; do you not perceive it? I am making a way in the desert and streams in the wasteland to give drink to my people, my chosen, the people I formed for myself that they may proclaim my praise. I say: My purpose will stand, and I will do all that I please.
What I have said, that will I bring about; what I have planned, that will I do."

—Isaiah 43:18–19, 20–21 and 46:10, 11

My doctor's eyes were full of compassion.

"The best thing for you is to go on the birth control pill," he said matter-of-factly.

Oh Lord, so this is it? Our fate is sealed? My thoughts swirled within me.

Conception will never be. No baby formed from us. No little life will stir in me. No long months of pregnancy. No labor. No delivery. Conception will never be.

Despite the years of unsuccessful trying, a glimmer of hope always flickered within me—that maybe, just maybe, it would happen one day.

But now aggravating cysts, wreaking havoc on my ovaries, could only be tamed by a tiny, little irony—an infertile woman on the birth control pill!

So, Lord, is this Your final answer?

With resignation, I accept this path.

Then a new idea is conceived; a new hope is formed in me. He is making a new way in the desert. His purpose stands! His plans prevail! He is still leading me!

And that is what my heart hoped for all along.

Bearing Fruit

If it weren't so sad, it would be funny—me, an "infertile" on birth control. But, you know, my body doesn't rule me. And despite what you may be feeling at the time, your body doesn't rule you, either. Do what's best for the overall good of your health. And trust in God that He is able to do a new thing in you.

Day
One Hundred Nineteen

Support System

Let us not give up meeting together, as some are
in the habit of doing,
but let us encourage one another—
and all the more as you see the Day approaching.
—Hebrews 10:25

My friend and I recently started an infertility support group at church. About seven couples attend our monthly meeting.

It's been amazing to see the slow but steady healing that's occurred as we've gleaned encouragement from others who have shared a similar burden. The men have especially benefited from this time together, maybe because guys often get less sympathy for their childlessness, though their pain and loss is no less real than a woman's.

When we meet, we generally discuss a book that we are all reading (currently it's *The Infertility Companion* by Sandra Glahn, Th.M., and William Cutrer, M.D.), and then have an "open mic" time where we vent our latest hurt, frustration, or struggle. And believe me, we each seem to have one or two!

I love this group. I feel a strong connection with each hurting member. Since God has so graciously led me to a place of greater contentment in my struggle with infertility, it stands to reason that I should make myself available to minister to others on this uniquely challenging journey.

No, we can't say *why* we are childless. We can only say that God is Sovereign, even in this circumstance. We can only say that we will not stop meeting together. We can only say that we will not give up.

Bearing Fruit

If there is an infertility support group in your area, consider attending. If that's not possible, consider connecting with others online. Try "Hannah's Prayer Community Forums Message Board Ministries" at www.hannah.org. Or try "Resolve: The National Infertility Association," at www.resolve.com. Sharing the pain lightens the load.

Day One Hundred Twenty

"I am Barren, but I Live."

"The righteous will flourish like a palm tree; they will grow like a cedar of Lebanon;
planted in the house of the Lord, they will flourish in the courts of our God.
They will still bear fruit in old age, they will stay fresh and green, proclaiming,
'The Lord is upright; he is my Rock, and there is no wickedness in him.'"

—Psalm 92:12–15

The pain of my barrenness hit me hard again. My friend was on the phone with her daughter, who was sharing the results of an ultrasound. It showed a little girl. I left the room to allow my friend the freedom to rejoice with her daughter.

And then it hit me.

I may never know that joy. In fact, it seems clear that I will indeed never know the joy of seeing my baby for the first time by ultrasound.

Even now as I attempt to put this into words, I am struck with grief.

A woman whose womb will never shelter a child feels a deep, untouchable pain. *Only tears can express what I feel.*

But this pain is only for a season: *I am barren right now, yet I will bear fruit again. The deadness I feel in my heart will pass into the hope of spring.*

What is the status of a tree that bears no fruit? Depends on the season. If it is winter, then the tree still lives, even though it is barren. But a tree that bears no fruit in spring or summer is dead.

I am alive. I will again bear spiritual fruit. This is but a season.

This is winter.

I am barren, but I live.

Bearing Fruit

Unexpected pain. It will surprise you time after time. But you can reduce recovery time. Even barren land can produce if it somehow gets water. God's Word gives that Living Water. You can flourish like a palm tree if planted in the house of the Lord. You are alive. You will bear fruit again in due season. Don't wither in your barrenness. Live for Him! Live life fully!

Day
One Hundred Twenty-One

Lead Me to the Promised Land

"If the Lord is pleased with us, he will lead us into that land, a land flowing with milk and honey, and will give it to us."

—Numbers 14:8

A fruitful life in a barren land—that's what I've found in the travels of my infertility journey. I'll never shake it off completely, though—the pain of childlessness. Reminders pop up daily.

However, being childless won't crush me. That's impossible as long as I stick close to the pathway as the Lord guides. I survey the carnage as I recall this journey....

There are dried tear stains, fixed cracks in a broken heart, healed scars from surgeries, unclenched fists after times of anger....

I rise from the rubble, from the collapse of this dream of motherhood, determined to build new dreams.

I bask in this Promised Land of peace and rest in relationship with my great Jehovah God—for He has led me here.

Bearing Fruit

Can there be a happy ending without a baby? Yes. Again, I say, yes! Whatever the cause of your childlessness, you can arrive at a place of contentment. Some find contentment in adoption. Some find it in pursuing the medical advances of fertility that sometimes result in a child. At this point, my husband and I have chosen to be childfree. But as you have seen in these pages, this doesn't mean our lives are devoid of children. Whatever path you choose, it will lead to contentment if you follow Great Jehovah God. He will guide you to the Promised Land—a land of peace. Lift your eyes toward the place of His leading. See Him there, beckoning you to follow. You can trust Him. You are not alone. Go, sister, go!

Follow the Romans Road

To begin your journey to eternal security with Jesus Christ, start here:

Romans 3:23:

For all have sinned and fall short of the glory of God....

Romans 6:23:

For the wages of sin is death, but the gift of God is eternal life in Christ Jesus our Lord.

Romans 5:8:

But God demonstrates his own love for us in this: While we were still sinners, Christ died for us.

Romans 10:9–10:

That if you confess with your mouth, "Jesus is Lord," and believe in your heart that God raised him from the dead, you will be saved. For it is with your heart that you believe and are justified, and it is with your mouth that you confess and are saved.

Romans 10:13:

Everyone who calls on the name of the Lord will be saved.

Infertility Decoder

ART: Assisted Reproductive Technology
LH: Luteinizing Hormone

HSG: Hysterosalpingogram
AIH: Artificial Insemination, Husband

BBT: Basal Body Temperature
IUI: Intrauterine Insemination

hCG: Human Chorionic Gonadotropin
IVF: In Vitro Fertilization

hMG: Human Menopausal Gonadotropin
GIFT: Gamete Intrafallopian Transfer

FSH: Follicle–stimulating Hormone
ZIFT: Zygote Intrafallopian Transfer

References

Schalesky, Marlo, *Empty Womb, Aching Heart*, p. 95.

Williams, William, *Guide Me, O Thou Great Jehovah.*

Chapman, Annie, *Smart Women Keep it Simple, (Quoting "In the Quiet of This Moment Prayer Journal," by Laurel Oke Logan)*

Chambers, Oswald, *My Utmost for His Highest*, July 6., September 4.

Bridwell, Debra, *The Ache for a Child*, p. 153.

Johnson, Patricia Irwin, *Adopting After Infertility*, p. 20.

Lutzer, Erwin, *One Minute After You Die*, p. 74.

Marsh, Margaret and Wanda Ronner, *The Empty Cradle: Infertility in America from Colonial*

Times to the Present, p. 64.

Spring, Beth, *Childless*, p. 30.

Smith, Hannah Whitall, *The Christian's Secret of a Happy Life*, p.160.

Benn, Gail, with permission.

Dake, Cindy Lewis, *Infertility: A Survival Guide for Couples and Those Who Love Them*, p. 217–218.

Smith, Hannah Whitall, *The Christian's Secret of a Happy Life*, p.45.

Ortberg, John, *The Life You Always Wanted*, p. 143.

Chambers, Oswald, *My Utmost for His Highest*, October 23.

Glahn, Sandra and William Cutrer, M.D., *When Empty Arms Become a Heavy Burden: Encouragement for Couples Facing Infertility*, p. 138–139, p. 143.

Frost, Robert, "*The Road Not Taken*"

Resources

Bridwell, Debra. *The Ache for a Child.* SP Publications, Inc., 1994.

Chambers, Oswald. *My Utmost for His Highest*, Updated Edition. Edited by James G. *Reimann. Oswald Chambers Publications Association, Ltd, 1992.*

Dake, Cindy Lewis *Infertility: A Survival Guide for Couples and Those Who Love Them.* New *Hope Publishers, 2002.*

Glahn, Sandra and William Cutrer, M.D. *When Empty Arms Become a Heavy Burden. Broadman & Holman Publishers, 1997.*

Glahn, Sandra, Th.M. and William Cutrer, M.D. *The Infertility Companion.* Zondervan *Publishing House, 2004.*

Johnson, Patricia Irwin. *Adopting After Infertility.* Perspectives Press, 1992.

Lutzer, Erwin W. *One Minute After You Die.* Moody Press, 1997.

Ortberg, John. *The Life You've Always Wanted.* Zondervan Publishing House, 1997.

Marsh, Margaret and Wanda Ronner. *The Empty Cradle.* John Hopkins University *Press, 1996.*

Schalesky, Marlo. *Empty Womb, Aching Heart.* Bethany House Publishers, 2001.

Smith, Hannah Whitall. *The Christian's Secret of a Happy Life.* Barbour and Company, *Inc., 1985.*

CPSIA information can be obtained at www.ICGtesting.com
265536BV00001B/2/A